# How to Increase
# Church Membership
# and Attendance

# How to Increase Church Membership and Attendance

Weldon Crossland

ABINGDON-COKESBURY PRESS
New York • Nashville

# HOW TO INCREASE CHURCH MEMBERSHIP
# AND ATTENDANCE

SET UP, PRINTED, AND BOUND BY THE PARTHENON PRESS, AT NASHVILLE, TENNESSEE, UNITED STATES OF AMERICA

# PREFACE

THIS book seeks to gather up the best in evangelistic planning and experience of hundreds of city, town, and country churches of many communions in America, and to give these features their proper place in the framework of a well-rounded program of a year of evangelism in the local church.

While most current forms of evangelism are considered, the accent is placed on these four chief areas of evangelistic opportunity, any one of which is worthy of an entire volume: pulpit evangelism, visitation evangelism, educational evangelism through the church school, and the re-evangelizing of the inactive, indifferent, nonattending members of the local church.

This handbook of basic principles and practical plans, written for the busy pastor and the active layman, presents the chief objectives, emphases, and techniques that will assure continuous evangelism through the church year.

Any church of any size anywhere that adapts and uses these tested plans will find its membership growing and its attendance increasing.

Especially helpful counsel and suggestions have been given by Dr. Harry Denman, Dr. Jesse M. Bader, and many others, to whom I give my cordial appreciation and thanks.

WELDON CROSSLAND

5

# CONTENTS

CHAPTER 1

# How to Plan a Year's
# Program of Evangelism

BASIC PRINCIPLES

1. Any church anywhere can greatly increase its membership and attendance through Christian evangelism.
2. All suitable methods of evangelism should be used.
3. The sermon, the church school, and home visitation evangelism offer the church its chief evangelistic opportunities.
4. Representative lay members must share as partners in all planning and work, with the minister as their leader and guide.
5. The reclaiming of inactive church members ranks with the winning of converts as a highly important evangelistic task.
6. A well-rounded program of evangelistic objectives and methods should be planned for the entire year.

THE good news of the Son of God must be set against the dark background of the world's tragic chaos and man's desperate personal need. Secularism is a slow poison that corrodes morality and destroys civilization. Militarism is a rigid vice whose steel jaws painfully grip mankind. Disillusionment is a contagious virus that kills the faith and hope by which men live. Frustration is a creeping paralysis that saps the strength

11

and courage of the soul. Mankind is sick, and men have lost their way.

The evangel of Jesus Christ offers the only sure hope of humanity today. It is the antidote to spiritual disease and death, the medicine of abundant life. Evangelism is the chief need of the world.

Christ has given us Christians the *mandate:* "Go ye into all the world, and preach the gospel to every creature." We have his saving *message:* "I am the way, the truth, and the life." We know his effective *methods:* "Ye shall be my witnesses." We have available ample *motivation* through the Spirit of God in each of us.

With these immortal tidings in our mortal hands we must go forth to conquer and to redeem the world.

Christian evangelism must never be identified with any one method or technique, nor be confused with the program or plans which it uses. These are but means to the end that all men may become Christian.

Laymen and ministers of a number of communions have defined evangelism as:

The bringing of men to Christ and Christ to men

Persuading people to accept Jesus Christ as their Lord and Saviour

The coming of the divine new life of God through faith in Christ into the life of the believer

Salvation from sin; redemption from evil through faith in Christ

Challenging men to obey Christ's command "Follow me"

Seeking and winning the lost to Christ and to the Christian way

Offering the rich, abundant, victorious life of Jesus Christ to men

Leading men into a vital, saving relationship to Jesus Christ.

Two more comprehensive and formal definitions or descriptions were formulated by the Foreign Missions Conference at Madras and by the World Council of Churches at Amsterdam, respectively:

By evangelism we understand that the Church Universal, in all its branches, and through the service of all its members, must so present Christ Jesus to the world in the power of the Holy Spirit that men shall come to put their trust in God through Him, accept Him as their Saviour and serve Him as their Lord in the fellowship of His Church.

To the Church, then, is given the privilege of so making Christ known to men that each is confronted with the necessity of a personal decision, Yes or No. The Gospel is the expression both of God's love to man, and of His claim to man's obedience. In this lies the solemnity of the decision. Those who obey are delivered from the power of the world in which sin reigns, and already, in the fellowship of the children of God, have the experience of eternal life. Those who reject the love of God remain under His judgment and are in danger of sharing in the impending doom of the world that is passing away.

**Understand and evaluate the new evangelism** which has come into being during the past twenty-five years. It is broader, richer, deeper, saner, and more comprehensive and effective than in any era since the Apostolic Age. It employs every worthy evangelistic method, becoming all things to all men in the spirit of Christ. It is a partnership between the minister and the laymen as they unite to witness for their living Lord. It uses the best educational techniques as well as valid emotional ones. It stresses the Christian Church as well as the Christian decision. It carefully trains all converts both before and after their decision. It accents assimilation into the Christian fellowship as well as commitment to Christ. It seeks the "lost sheep of the house of Israel" —inactive and nonresident church members—as well as those who have never become Christians. It has a keen sense of responsibility for the redemption of its community as well as the saving of individuals. And it heightens its effectiveness by encouraging unified, interchurch evangelistic crusades on a community-wide basis.

There are many kinds of evangelism now being used successfully by the Christian communions of America. Among today's valid and varied methods of bringing souls into the kingdom of God through faith in Jesus Christ as Lord and Saviour are these:

1. *Pulpit evangelism,* where through sermon and worship in the regular church services converts are won and indifferent Christians reclaimed to a loving loyalty to Jesus Christ.

2. *Educational evangelism,* which uses teaching techniques in the church school, the youth groups, and other organizations, that personalities may grow in grace and in the knowledge of the truth as it is in Christ Jesus our Lord.

3. *Personal evangelism,* which is the winning of individuals for Christ by individual Christians.

4. *Visitation evangelism,* through the organized choosing, training, and sending out of selected workers in teams of two, as Jesus did the Twelve and the Seventy.

5. *Public evangelism* in preaching missions or evangelistic services, where conversions and rededications are sought.

6. *Clinical evangelism,* through counseling and conversation.

7. *Child and youth evangelism,* where life in its most plastic, impressionable period is claimed for Christ and his church.

8. *Group evangelism* in a lodge, grange, or labor union, by which the group and its program become progressively Christian.

9. *Social evangelism,* through a community-wide crusade against those evils which secularize and corrupt human life.

10. *Communications evangelism,* through radio, television, newspapers, and tracts as the important mediums of expression.

11. *Family evangelism,* where the attitudes and activities of family life become more and more Christlike through daily devotions, family worship, grace at meals, and religious conversation.

12. *Fellowship evangelism,* which seeks to plant and to nurture the prospective convert in the life and spirit of the Christian fellowship *before* inviting him to become a Christian and a member of the church.

13. *Cell evangelism,* where a small group of six to twelve Christians and non-Christians meet to discuss Christ and the Christian way of living for the enrichment of their own lives and the winning of converts.

It is fascinating to note that every one of these successful, modern techniques was used in its first-century form by Jesus in his matchless ministry. What Christ has joined together, in a well-rounded program of Christian evangelism, let no man put asunder. While no one church will employ all these evangelistic methods, each church will use several of them, accenting the visitation, educational, and preaching types, from which over 90 per cent of the converts and new members come.

It is deeply gratifying to note that the word "evangelism," which suffered for a time from certain emotional and financial abuses, is today deservedly growing in favor, acceptability, and use in every Christian communion in America.

**Think through your evangelistic problems.** As commander in chief the minister, with his lay associates, must choose the evangelistic objective, plan the campaign, train the workers, provide the ammunition, assign the forces, lead the attack, and consolidate the victory. He is Christ's chief man in this holy warfare. He must think clearly, realistically, and creatively concerning the extension of Christ's kingdom. His leadership and kindling enthusiasm will vitalize the entire evangelistic movement and will assure high success. In considering the twelve-months program of evangelism for his church, he will raise, among others, these questions:

How many new members joined our church last year?

How many of these were received on the confession of their faith?

Is this number more or less than 5.6 per cent of our membership, which for most churches is the dividing line between growth and decline?

How many names of prospects are now on our responsibility roll?

How can this list be greatly increased?

How can I make my sermons more evangelistic?

Would not a preaching mission or public evangelistic services be beneficial to my church?

How can the indifferent, nonattending members of our church be reclaimed to a new loyalty?

What membership and attendance goals would Christ have our church set?

When should the visitation evangelism crusade be held?

Should this visitation crusade, the church attendance movement, and the friendly community study or census be held on a community-wide basis in close co-operation with other churches and ministers?

How much instruction should converts and the children and youth of a membership training class receive?

How often should new members be welcomed into our church?

How can I make the service of reception more impressive?

How can our church build new members more securely and permanently into our fellowship?

How can the committee on membership and evangelism be enlarged and strengthened?

Should not some young people and church-school teachers be added to this committee?

When and where should this committee meet to plan a well-rounded program of evangelism for the church year?

What important matters should be discussed at this meeting?

How can I lead my people into a deeper concern for souls and a year-round sharing of their faith in Christ with others?

**Organize a committee on membership and evangelism.** Since evangelism is a co-operative task shared by pastor and people, the wise minister will next discuss with tact and enthusiasm the evangelistic record and opportunity of his church with his evangelistic chairman. If the minister is incompetent or stupid, he will lay before his chairman a completed program of evangelism for the year. No better method was ever invented to stultify lay thinking, to undermine lay leadership, to dampen lay enthusiasm, and to ensure failure than this one. If, however, the pastor is a competent and effective leader, he will do a fine piece of co-operative kingdom planning with the chairman by outlining the high importance of evangelism in the work of the church, and then by inviting and drawing out the ideas and comments of the chairman, whose chief position in evangelism ranks next to that of the minister. With his background of professional training and wide experience he can easily raise questions, offer suggestions and counsel concerning methods, in such a way that the chairman's knowledge, interests, and sense of responsibility will be heightened.

Because the church of tomorrow will largely be determined by the type of church members received today, the ablest and most representative members of the congregation should be appointed to the membership and evangelism committee. The strengthening and enlargement of this committee in the average church is necessary in order that it might include representative officials, such as the superintendent of the church school, the president of the women's organization, and certain outstanding youth leaders.

The entire membership of the enlarged committee should then be called together for an evening of planning and program building, preferably at the manse or parsonage. As presiding officer the chairman will ask for suggestions and encourage free discussion by everyone present. The minister will offer his counsel and guidance in the decisions of the committee. An "order of business" in question form may well include the following:

1. What is evangelism, and why is it important to our church?

2. How well did we do our evangelistic task last year?

3. What are the evangelistic opportunities before our church this coming year?

4. How many prospective members are there now on our constituency roll?

5. What goals should we set for the coming year (a) in converts, (b) in new members for our church, and (c) in church attendance?

6. Shall we hold the church loyalty movement to re-interest and reclaim our indifferent members? When?

7. Shall we sometime during the year hold a visitation evangelism crusade and special evangelistic services? When?

8. Should our church, in co-operation with other churches of the community, hold a friendly community study or census to discover the names of children, young people, and adults who are not in any church or church school?

9. What other features should be included in the evangelistic calendar of emphases and events for the year?

10. When shall our committee meet again to discuss its important work?

The month-by-month program for the evangelistic year outlined at the close of this chapter will be helpful to the chairman, minister, and any committees appointed, as they plan and carry out their work.

**Plan to go to the people.** The church that merely announces its services with the expectation that people will come as they are alleged to have done in former years is in for a large measure of disappointment and failure. Except in extremely unusual circumstances the people simply will not come. To win converts and to enlist new members a congregation must "go out into the highways and byways and compel them to come in." Only by calling on them in their homes and offices can they be persuaded to enter the Lord's house and worship with his people. Without organized, effective visitation there is no worthy increase in church membership or attendance.

There are no doubt many unchurched children, young people, and adults in your community. The evangelistic task of any church must be seen against the somber background of more than seventy million people in America who are not in any church or synagogue and twenty million children and young people who receive little or no religious instruction. Millions of these are unchurched Christians who count themselves followers of Christ, but who have never brought their certificate of membership to any church in the community where they reside. In scores of communities, large and small, where careful census surveys have been made, the number of these "lost church members" exceeds the total recorded church membership of the community. The non-Christians number tens of millions, while the children and young people outside the church and church school outnumber those who receive adequate moral and religious training. These groups constitute a ringing challenge and rich opportunity for an aggressive evangelistic program in every Christian church.

The friendly community study or census, conducted co-operatively by all the churches of the community, has been found to be the best possible technique for discovering the names and addresses of unchurched persons in any city or town. Such a city-wide Christian movement attracts favorable attention, while the newspapers, recognizing its publicity value, give it generous news coverage. Churches find it easier to enlist workers for such an interchurch effort, while this definite demonstration of Christian unity is not lost on the community. The churches cannot possibly do their full evangelistic task without such a census every two or three years. Census cards, training folders, and other materials suitable for such an interdenominational census study may be procured from any of the leading denominations.

One of the most important evangelistic tasks, which the new evangelism accents, is that of reclaiming the indifferent, inactive, nonattending, and nonresident members of the church. In some churches those who have lost interest, and who habitually absent themselves from the services, number from one third to one half of the total membership. Most of these fail to support the church in any way through their gifts or through their service. They are the "lost sheep" who must be brought back to the fold. Others are among the tens of millions of Americans who have changed their residence in these recent nomadic years. They must be faithfully followed up and related to a church in their new community, or they will in all likelihood be lost to the church.

**Outline a program of evangelistic emphases.** Any activity as vital to the well-being of the church as is evangelism deserves the advantages that come from long-range planning. Any church of any size anywhere should include these twelve projects, among others, if it would do its God-given evangelistic task in a worthy manner:

An evangelistic spirit and aim in the Sunday sermons and services

An up-to-date responsibility roll of nonmembers and inactive members of the church

A challenging goal in the number of new members to be received and in the number of worshipers attending church

A church-wide loyalty crusade in the early autumn for increased church and church-school attendance

A friendly community study or census once every two or three years

A visitation evangelism crusade in which the church school shares

Membership training or confirmation classes for children, young people, and adults

A preaching mission or special evangelistic services

An impressive reception of all new members as often as is desirable

A plan for assimilating new members and reclaimed members into the active life of the church

A fellowship of evangelism for continuous evangelistic calling

An earnest request for church-wide faith, prayer, and cooperation in the evangelistic program of the church.

Each of these important phases of evangelistic endeavor is described in detail in the following chapters.

Increasing thousands of churches are coming to outline their evangelistic objectives, emphases, and events on a twelve-months basis, in this way avoiding the chaos and inefficiency of haphazard, shortsighted planning. Nearly all the communions in America today prepare constructive outlines of objectives and projects in evangelism for the guidance and help of their churches through the church or calendar year. The following program for the church year in evangelism, which includes many of the best features of these denominational outlines, can easily be adapted to the needs of large or small churches of any communion anywhere.

## I. THE PERIOD OF RETURN AND RECOVERY

SEPTEMBER

*1st Week*        Plan and organize a church loyalty crusade of friendly visitation to call on every member of the church, especially on the inactive, indifferent members to persuade them to promise:

1. To take communion on World Communion Sunday, which is the first Sunday in October
2. To share in the church loyalty movement, to be launched October 1, by being present in church every Sunday
3. To become a member of some church-school class for fellowship, study, and service
4. To pray daily for the world, for one's church, and for one's self.

Use the Sunday-evening service as an opportunity for evangelism and fellowship.

*3rd Week*        Launch the church loyalty crusade.

*4th Sunday*    RALLY DAY–CHRISTIAN EDUCATION SUNDAY in the church and church school.

OCTOBER

*1st Sunday*    WORLD COMMUNION SUNDAY—"Every Christian taking communion."

First Sunday of the church loyalty crusade, with its challenge to every member to a deeper Christian loyalty and to every-Sunday church attendance.

Reception of new members.

*2nd Sunday*    The second Sunday of the church loyalty crusade.

Preaching mission or evangelistic services for one or two weeks—or at some other time of the year as desired.

*3rd Week*    Preparations for the visitation evangelism crusade to open the second Sunday in November and to climax on Ingathering Sunday, the first Sunday in December. Some ministers prefer to hold this crusade during Lent or at some other period in the year. Invite the co-operation of the Board of Education in this crusade with "every teacher an evangelist."

*4th Sunday*    REFORMATION SUNDAY, an opportunity to bear the Protestant Christian witness.

Fourth Sunday of the church loyalty crusade.

## II. LOOKING TOWARD THE ADVENT SEASON

NOVEMBER

*1st Week*    Completion of all plans for the visitation evangelism crusade.

2nd Sunday — Launching of the visitation evangelism crusade for the winning of converts and new members, continuing through Monday, Tuesday, and Wednesday.

3rd Sunday — Formation of the "fellowship of evangelism" for continuous evangelism, composed of the most effective workers in the visitation evangelism crusade.

4th Sunday — THANKSGIVING SUNDAY
World-Wide Bible-Reading Movement— Thanksgiving to Christmas.
The membership training class.

## DECEMBER

1st Sunday — INGATHERING SUNDAY for the welcoming of converts and new members into the fellowship of the church.

2nd Sunday — UNIVERSAL BIBLE SUNDAY

3rd Sunday — CHRISTMAS SUNDAY
The baptism of children.

25th — CHRISTMAS DAY

31st — Watch-night candlelight service of communion and rededication.

## III. THE NEW YEAR OPENS

### JANUARY

1st Sunday — NEW YEAR'S SUNDAY OR RECONSECRATION SUNDAY, with its accent on spiritual enrichment and Christlike living.
Urge every-Sunday attendance by every member through Easter.
Reception of new members.
The Sunday evening service is an opportunity for evangelism and fellowship.

2nd Week        Meeting of church committee on member-
                ship and evangelism to discuss the com-
                ing Lenten period and other evangelistic
                opportunities.

                Plan and prepare for Decision Day in the
                church school, if one is desired, in co-
                operation with the board of education
                and the teachers.

4th Sunday      DECISION DAY in the church school.

FEBRUARY

1st Sunday      The membership training or confirmation
                class to hold its first session, continuing
                each week to Palm Sunday, or better, to
                Pentecost Sunday.

                Reception of new members.

2nd Week        Make definite plans for the visitation evan-
                gelism crusade, to be held the third week
                in Lent—or at some other time—begin-
                ning on the third Sunday of March and
                climaxing with Palm Sunday as Ingather-
                ing Sunday.

## IV. THE LENTEN SEASON [1]

1st Wednesday   ASH WEDNESDAY service of meditation, self-
                examination, self-denial, and communion.

1st Sunday      FIRST SUNDAY IN LENT. The beginning of
                a series of seven sermons on the great
                fundamentals of our Christian faith and
                life or some other appropriate theme.

                Stress the Christian duty and privilege of

[1] Because the date of Easter changes from year to year, the Lenten
program of evangelism has been set in the framework of the months
March and April. The adjustments of the features of the Lenten
program to the correct date each year is a simple matter.

being present at church every Sunday in Lent.

Reception of new members.

2nd Sunday    SECOND SUNDAY IN LENT. All plans and personnel for the visitation evangelism crusade should be completed by this date.

3rd Sunday    THIRD SUNDAY IN LENT. Launching of the visitation evangelism crusade for the winning of converts and new members.

4th Sunday    FOURTH SUNDAY IN LENT

APRIL

1st Sunday    FIFTH SUNDAY IN LENT

Preaching mission or evangelistic services for one or two weeks, or at some other period of the year as desired.

2nd Sunday    SIXTH SUNDAY IN LENT, PALM SUNDAY

INGATHERING DAY for the reception of new members, including those from the membership or confirmation class of the church school.

Baptism of children.

HOLY WEEK services open.

HOLY THURSDAY service of Communion.

GOOD FRIDAY services.

3rd Sunday    EASTER DAY [2]

The reception of any new members who could not be present on Palm Sunday.

[2] The dates of Easter through 1970 are as follows:

| 1950 | April 9 | 1957 | April 21 | 1964 | March 29 |
|------|---------|------|----------|------|----------|
| 1951 | March 25 | 1958 | April 6 | 1965 | April 18 |
| 1952 | April 13 | 1959 | March 29 | 1966 | April 10 |
| 1953 | April 5 | 1960 | April 17 | 1967 | March 26 |
| 1954 | April 18 | 1961 | April 2 | 1968 | April 14 |
| 1955 | April 10 | 1962 | April 22 | 1969 | April 6 |
| 1956 | April 1 | 1963 | April 14 | 1970 | March 29 |

3rd Week       The thorough assimilation of all new mem-
               bers, by calling, pledging, and actively
               relating each one to the appropriate class
               of the church school and to other suitable
               groups.

## V. THE PERIOD OF PENTECOST

MAY

2nd Sunday     MOTHER'S DAY, FESTIVAL OF THE CHRISTIAN
               HOME
               Accent the Christianization of the home
               through the Christian family movement
               or some similar project.
               Baptism of children.

4th Sunday     MEMORIAL SUNDAY (may be 5th Sunday)

JUNE

1st Sunday     PENTECOST SUNDAY, [3] "The Birthday of the
               Church."
               Reception of new members.

3rd Week       Meeting of the committee on membership
               and evangelism to plan the evangelistic
               program for the twelve months beginning
               September 1.
               Strengthen both the committee on member-
               ship and evangelism and the fellowship
               of evangelism for the work of the com-
               ing year.

## VI. THE SUMMER SEASON

JULY AND AUGUST

               Summer evangelistic services.
               The daily vacation Bible school to be held

[3] The date of Pentecost Sunday will change each year with the date
of Easter.

> to serve the children of the community.
> Institute and retreat for young people and adults.
> Youth caravan for community service and evangelism.

*Believe! Pray! Work!*

Since the day of Pentecost faith, prayer, and witnessing have been the chief channels through which the power of the spirit of God has flowed with evangelistic blessing into the lives of individuals and nations.

A planned program for the year in evangelism, conceived in faith, undergirded with prayer, and glorified with work will bring a rich and inevitable harvest. It will also solve many of the difficult problems, such as new leadership and finance, which perplex church leaders everywhere.

> Pray as if everything depended on God,
> Work as if everything depended on you.
> —IGNATIUS

# CHAPTER 2

# How to Make
# Preaching Evangelistic

BASIC PRINCIPLES

1. The pulpit offers every minister his greatest evangelistic opportunity.

2. Sermons that evangelize can be preached by any minister in any church anywhere.

3. A sermon is evangelistic when its chief, dynamic purpose is a favorable commitment, either public or private, to Christ and to the Christian way of life.

4. The most helpful evangelistic sermons as a rule will be those preached to a congregation by its own minister.

5. An opportunity for personal counsel and guidance should always be given.

6. The preaching mission holds rich possibilities for deepening church loyalty, as do special evangelistic services for securing converts.

IT is impossible to overestimate the power and influence of the gospel on the lips of a minister who preaches for a verdict. "The hour of decision becomes the hour of destiny." When Dwight L. Moody preached one evening in London, Wilfred Grenfell determined to devote his life to the fisherfolk of Labrador. When John R. Mott spoke with deep earnestness of the open doors of missionary opportunity, college students in great numbers became student volunteers. When Bishop Theodore S. Henderson preached on "Whatever, Whenever, Wherever, Pleases Him," hundreds of us dedicated our lives to full-time Christian service. And when Peter preached on the day of Pentecost, "the same day there were added unto them about three thousand souls."

The most important single task of any minister is to preach the good news of the Son of God and his kingdom to his congregation at the hour of public worship. In scope, creativity, and spiritual achievement no other opportunity for Christian service can equal it. Christianity at its best has always used the sermon as a chief means of proclaiming Christian truths and of challenging men to a dedication or rededication of their lives to Jesus Christ.

**Evaluate evangelistic preaching.** The addresses, lectures, orations, discourses, essays, pronouncements, and messages which by common courtesy pass for sermons differ radically in content, purpose, and spirit from the sermons that can honestly be called evangelistic. Whether preached as the "regular" sermon at a Sunday service or at a revival meeting, a sermon may properly be called evangelistic when it:

Proclaims that God has given Jesus Christ to men, and that men must accept this divine Gift if they are to be saved.

Offers an abundant, victorious life to all who accept Christ.

Promises redemption from sin, selfishness, fear, and all the enemies of the soul, through faith in Christ.

Commends God's way through Christ as the only answer to the problems of the world.

Urges enlistment under the banner of Christ and commitment to him as Lord and Saviour.

There is a clear note of urgency sounded in every evangelistic sermon. It appeals for decision and commitment. It possesses faith and fervor. It pleads for a verdict for Jesus Christ. It witnesses to the power of God which comes through faith in Christ. Because it is desperately in earnest, the evangelistic sermon strives to bring men to Christ and Christ to men.

**Preach for a verdict.** The chief aim of every minister as he preaches his sermon should be similar to that of the conscientious lawyer who pleads the case of his client in the courtroom—the winning of a favorable verdict. The gospel is good news of God, and it is a high privilege and duty to bring that divine message with such persuasive earnestness that men will believe and obey. The minister will turn the spotlight of God's Word, the Bible, on man's disorder in the light of God's design. Whether he preaches about God as a personal friend, Christ as a divine redeemer, faith as a creative power, religion as a heartwarming joy, service as a way of abundant living, or death and everlasting life as glorious adventures, he will seek above everything, not the praise of his congregation, but their wholehearted commitment to the great cause he has presented.

He may challenge Christians to more Christlike daily living. He may rebuke the sinner and call him to repentance and salvation. He may seek to win the non-Christian to the Christian way of life. He may challenge the church member to a deeper loyalty to Jesus Christ. He may claim the life of youth for Christian service. He may enlist the worshiper in the campaign of world redemption to Christian missions. He may plead for a higher loyalty on the part of the congregation to Christ and his Church.

The minister's own personal witness, in which he will

always avoid spiritual pride or boasting on the one hand and a timid, sensitive, false modesty on the other, will sound the authentic note of personal conviction as he preaches. One resourceful preacher, whose sermons always sound a strong, sane evangelistic note, often announces before his Sunday-morning sermon that at the close of the service he will give all who desire to start the Christian life or unite with the church the opportunity to do so. "I find that God richly blesses me, while his Spirit works in the consciences and hearts of many people as I preach."

In any public service worship and witness are inseparable.

The strategic place of the "moment of decision" in the Christian life should be realized. While many sermons to which congregations patiently listen are too often chance shots in the twilight at a target only dimly seen, the evangelistic sermon drives toward a favorable decision and an affirmative vote. This decision may be made silently in the soul of the listener in the pew as he accepts Christ and pledges him a life of love and loyalty. He may find Christ by coming forward to the altar, finding there forgiveness and new life as he kneels before God. His commitment may occur in the counsel room as he and the minister explore the glorious redemption that comes through faith in the Son of God. Although the manner and place of conversion may differ according to the temperament, training, and background of each convert, all have the unmistakable mark of God's loving approval.

There should be an appeal for a Christian decision. Using persuasion rather than pressure the preacher-evangelist will select those appeals he judges most effective and will phrase them in his own challenging yet winsome words. Among the one-sentence appeals that have been successfully used are these:

Accept God's great plan for your life.
Follow Christ and his way of life.
Bring your life into line with the high purposes of God.
Give Christ your love, your loyalty, and your allegiance.
Let Christ take care of all the fears, hate, sickness, and frustrations that plague your life.
Make Christ and loyalty to him the center of your life.
Begin a new way of life now in partnership with the Son of God.
With Christ's help you can be free from your sins and evil habits.
Begin today your friendship with the divine Friend.
Let God's power transform and strengthen your life.

The substance of two somewhat longer challenges are as follows:

My friends, Christ can gloriously save you from all the emptiness, frustration, futility, and despair that rob you of real living. You thought you had freedom as you went your own way. You found it often rough and bitter. In your own strength you failed, as I have so often in mine. Christ wants to help you. He wants you to achieve the noblest possible in glorious living. Through him alone you can find the highest meaning of Christ. Your faith in him will unite you with his unlimited power, and you will find that you can do all things through Christ, who strengthens you. Shift the center of your life to him! Organize your life about Jesus Christ! He is God's answer to your every need. Accept him and follow him!

I am asking you tonight to enlist in the army of the Lord. I am urging you to declare your allegiance to him and to enroll under his victorious banner. He is the generalissimo of the soul, the leader and commander of all good men.

Alone you have not a chance in the world to win. With him you will be victorious through your conquering faith in him. With him you will see active service as you help him free all mankind. Become a Christian now through your pledge of love and allegiance to him!

Sermon titles can have an evangelistic flavor. Some sermonic themes naturally lend themselves to evangelistic preaching and appeal. They arouse interest, stir the imagination, and challenge the reason and will to action. From the minds and hearts of many American preachers have come the following subjects which ably express the evangelistic motive:

> Every Man's Life a Plan of God
> How to Become a Christian
> Three Steps to God
> What Christ Does for Men
> What Jesus Means to Me
> Do We Really Want God?
> The Secret of Victorious Living
> Christ Has All the Answers
> You Belong to God
> This Life Is Worth Living
> Beyond the Old Frontiers
> If Christ Had Not Come
> God and Man's Need
> What Is God Doing Now?
> The Church and the World
> For Christ and His Church
> Eventually—Why Not Now?
> Begin Living Today
> The Power to See It Through
> What Will You Do with Jesus?
> Our God Is Able
> The Ultimate Question

Why Not Try Christ's Way?
What Think Ye of Christ?
In Partnership with God
Life and How to Build It

**Plan a preaching mission or special evangelistic services.** Combining old values that should never have been lost with new titles and techniques that have proved successful, public evangelism under such names as "The Preaching Mission" or "The Preaching-Teaching Mission" has been rightly accorded a prominent place in the evangelistic vocabulary and technique of America's Christian churches. After years of disuse because of certain limitations and abuses, the time-honored method of public evangelism is fortunately returning to favor among increasing thousands of ministers and churches. Out of such highly effective movements as the National Preaching Mission and the National Christian Mission has come a new type of pastor-evangelist, numbering into the hundreds, who is able to lead churches into the rich experiences of this modern form of public evangelism.

The preaching mission is not just a streamlined, repainted old model of the ancient "revival service" or "protracted meeting." It is a new kind of mass and group evangelism richer in content, more varied in method, and broader in appeal. It is a carefully planned evangelistic movement in a local church or on a community-wide basis, which through a series of public services undergirds and supplements the evangelistic objectives of the church.

Chief among its varied purposes are these:

1. To deepen and enrich the spiritual life of the church.

2. To win new converts to Jesus Christ.

3. To reclaim inactive, indifferent church members to a renewed loyalty.

4. To bridge the gap between the church and its neighborhood.

5. To guide Christians into the fellowship of the church.

6. To Christianize and spiritualize the lives of all who live in the community.

In its endeavor to achieve these high aims it enlists the best in worship, music, preaching, publicity, evangelistic appeal, and personal witness.

The spiritual success of any preaching mission will be largely determined by the care and thoroughness expended in preparing for it. Because the mission has so many competitors, such as scheduled community events, motion pictures, radio, and television, long-term preparation and intensive promotion are indispensable to success. A large number of the loyal members of the church must be organized into active committees responsible for such matters as attendance, publicity, music, special features, ushering, invited groups, visitation of prospective converts, calling on inactive members, and assimilation. Let there be:

*Earnest prayer* by individuals and groups that God will prosper and bless the mission.

*Painstaking planning* of all phases of the movement.

*Eager expectation* that the mission will be a great success.

*Attractive announcements* from the pulpit, among the church organizations, and in the calendar.

*Persuasive publicity* in the public press, through cards and handbills, and, if possible, by radio announcement.

*Letters of invitation* mailed to all church members and constituents.

*Personal invitation* by church members and friends.

*Appropriate announcements* of any special features such as special nights and music.

*Personal visitation* of prospective converts and indifferent members.

*Inspiring messages* preached by the minister or the guest missioner for a verdict.

*Faith and assurance* on the part of all that God will crown all worthy efforts with success.

When these methods were used for the recent seven-day preaching mission in the Cathedral of St. John the Divine in New York City—a city not noted for its eager response to evangelism—42,500 Episcopalians and their friends attended, with over 600 seeking the inquiry room after the service on a single evening.

The length of a preaching mission will range all the way from one week to three or four. One week of intensive evangelistic effort, from one Sunday morning until the evening of the following Sunday, provides the average church with an adequate period of evangelistic opportunity and spiritual adventure. Many ministers and guest preachers will feel that one week is not long enough to sow the seed, cultivate the field, and reap the harvest. While the date chosen will be determined by local conditions, one of the weeks of the October church loyalty crusade, the first week in the new year, the opening week of Lent, Holy Week, or the week including Pentecost Sunday are among those usually chosen.

The sermon subjects selected for any preaching mission will be determined largely by the purposes which the minister and the church desire to achieve. The accent may be on winning new converts, or on reclaiming inactive members, or on deepening the religious life of the church, with other objectives as supplemental. Under the general topic *What It Means to Be a Christian* the following subjects were the themes used in one successful preaching mission for the two Sundays and the five week-day evenings:

> How Shall We Think of God?
> Who Is Jesus Christ?
> The Christian Way of Life
> How to Become a Christian
> What Christ Expects of Every Christian
> How to Pray
> What Is the Christian Church?
> Why Every Christian Should Join the Church
> A Growing Christian

Every message delivered during the preaching mission ought to possess the note of persuasive, winsome urgency which characterizes every good evangelistic sermon.

**Secure attendance through individual workers.** Effective personal work is of inestimable value in helping achieve the high purposes of the preaching mission. It starts the prospective Christian thinking about religious matters. It encourages him to give serious consideration to his privilege and his duty. It confronts him with the claims of Jesus Christ. It persuasively urges him to be present at the services. It heightens the probability that he will make a favorable decision. While the training of personal workers here will not be as elaborate as the plan outlined in Chapters 3, 4, 5, and 9, it should include enough of the essential instructions to enable the visitor to make an effective call.

More than announcements, publicity, and prayer is required if the preaching mission is to secure the largest possible attendance and the highest success. The services must have the definite pledged support of large numbers of the church membership and constituency. The most effective and satisfactory attendance builder is the signed promise of scores or hundreds of people, who can easily be persuaded to give their loyal support to the mission by signing such a card as the following:

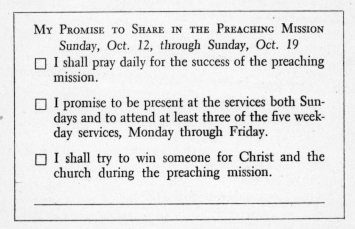

MY PROMISE TO SHARE IN THE PREACHING MISSION
*Sunday, Oct. 12, through Sunday, Oct. 19*
☐ I shall pray daily for the success of the preaching mission.

☐ I promise to be present at the services both Sundays and to attend at least three of the five weekday services, Monday through Friday.

☐ I shall try to win someone for Christ and the church during the preaching mission.

Many ministers urge the signing of this card at the church and church-school services on the two Sundays before the mission opens, in this way making it necessary for visitors to call only on those members of the church who have not made their promise.

**Invite counsel after each service.** The ancient mourner's bench, where the evangelist prayed and pleaded with the unsaved, has been replaced by the counsel room, where at the close of each service the preacher has a superb opportunity for conference with those who have chosen, or would like to choose, the Christian way of life. The skilled minister can creatively guide the lives and consciences of those who desire to understand and accept Jesus Christ, as he advises the perplexed, hears the confession of the sinner, and receives the commitment of the convert. His conference with them will be similar in spirit and content to the spiritual guidance visit of the pastor as described in Chapter 7.

The depth and permanence of the Christian life of those won through the preaching mission will be largely determined—as in every kind of evangelism—by the care and thoroughness with which they are related to the fellowship of Christ and his church through a wise program of assimilation.

# Chapter 3

# How to Organize
# a Visitation Evangelism Crusade

Basic Principles

1. **Visitation evangelism, which is personal work by trained laymen, was a favorite evangelistic method of Jesus.**

2 **Visitation evangelism will secure more decisions for Christ and his church than any other evangelistic method.**

3. **The ablest members of the church should be chosen and enlisted for the evangelistic task.**

4. **An up-to-date responsibility roll of prospective members is indispensable to success.**

5. **More than fifty per cent of those on this prospect list can be won by laymen.**

6. **Sharing in a visitation evangelism crusade is always a memorable Christian experience for pastor and people.**

VISITATION evangelism as a method is more than nineteen hundred years old. Jesus used it first as a favorite technique of witnessing, both for himself and his followers. He interviewed Zacchaeus in his home; Matthew at his office; Peter, Andrew, James, and John at their work; and the woman of Samaria at Jacob's well. After he had carefully chosen and trained the Twelve and the Seventy, he sent them out in teams of two to proclaim the kingdom and to persuade men to accept him as the Messiah. They returned radiant with joy, glorying in their amazing success, exactly as Christian evangelistic workers do today.

The genius of the visitation evangelism movement lies in the fact that qualified lay workers, carefully chosen and trained, take the good news of Christ and his church to people where they are. Tens of millions of the unsaved and unchurched people of America never enter a church. They ignore the regular services of worship and are cold to preaching missions and special evangelistic services. They can be reached for Christ only as loyal Christians go out into their homes and places of business, and by persuasion "compel them to come in." Most of the periods in Christian history that have recorded the largest spiritual growth and the greatest numerical advance have been those in which devoted laymen took the gospel to the people.

Laymen quickly grasp the unlimited possibilities of such evangelistic work and eagerly accept its adventurous challenge. "This is the most satisfying and worthwhile work I have ever done for Christ and my church," exclaimed a doctor, who with his wife as his teammate had secured seven decisions during a visitation crusade. They deepened their own faith in Christ as they commended him and his way of life to others. They strengthened their own loyalty to his Church as they persuaded others to unite with the Christian fellowship. Their hearts were "strangely warmed" as they won a convert or reclaimed a wandering Christian for Christ.

To determine the value and permanence of visitation evangelism one has only to look at the record. During the "Year of Evangelism" The Methodist Church won more than one million new members, about 65 per cent secured through visitation evangelism. In an Episcopal church of just over two hundred communicants, thirty-two evangelistic visitors in teams of two made this enviable record by persistent effort through the year: baptisms, fifty-five; confirmations, forty-three; transfers, sixty-two; and the phenomenal growth of the church school to more than two hundred. A widely known Illinois industrialist who served as chairman of the visitation crusade displayed justifiable pride as he related the following: "Our minister was ill for eight months last year. We laymen took hold of evangelism, and on Easter we had the largest class our church has ever known—137 new members. Our pastor didn't win a single one of them because he was flat on his back. He prayed, and we laymen did the work."

In thousands of communities, ranging from the congested cities to the open country, laymen have shown that they can use the visitation method with the highest of success. They persuade on the average more than 40 per cent of the adults they visit to make a favorable Christian decision, while about 99 per cent of the teams that faithfully attend the training conferences and call on all their prospects win one or more to Christ and his church. Surprisingly enough they secure a higher percentage of decisions than do the ministers themselves!

Reliable statistics show that there is little or no difference in matters of loyalty and permanence between those who make their decision in public evangelistic services and those who make their commitment to Christ in a visitation evangelism interview. The care and thoroughness with which the new Christian is assimilated into the life of the church far outrank the manner or place of his decision in determining the permanence of his interest in the church. After the passing of one year the converts of either major method of evangelism show that with an adequate plan for building them into the life of the church almost 95 per cent of them remain loyal.

Among the chief steps that are usually taken in planning and launching a personal evangelism crusade are the following:

1. **Secure supplies proportionate to your membership.** You can get training folders, visitation agreement cards, prospect and assignment cards, assignment envelopes, and record-of-decision cards from your denominational board of membership and evangelism. Every communion in America now makes available all the supplies that any church requires, in attractive form and practically at cost. A church of two hundred members should order about:

> One hundred prospect and assignment cards
> Twenty visitation agreement cards
> Fifty assignment and report envelopes
> Twenty-five each of the two or three instruction and training folders
> One hundred record-of-decision cards

The total cost of this printed material will amount to about three dollars. Churches can easily scale their orders for evangelistic literature according to their size.

2. **Make a responsibility roll of prospects.** An up-to-date prospect list—sometimes called a responsibility or constituency roll—is indispensable to any successful evangelistic effort. On this alphabetical master list should appear the name, address, and known information of every nonmember of the church who in any way looks to the church for any Christian service, or for whom the church should feel responsible in her community-

wide ministry. Since over fifty per cent of these prospects, whose number ought to equal one third of the membership of the church, can be won by laymen, the size of this responsibility roll will have an important relation to the growth of church membership across the years. In assembling the names of all who should be on the prospect list, the minister and those whom he chooses to assist him will find the following to be the chief sources:

*a*) *The church school.* The attendance record of the adult, young-adult, and youth departments will yield the names of many excellent prospects. The parents of the boys and girls in the children's division, including the nursery or cradle roll, rank among the best prospective members, since they are accepting the educational services of the church.

*b*) *Relatives of church members.* Husbands, wives, sisters, and brothers of church members—the "in-laws" of the church—are far more numerous than is generally suspected. Most of them can be claimed for Christ and his church, as is proved by the record of one Michigan minister who, in his regular calling during his first year, won over one hundred new members from this single source.

c) *Attendance registration*. In most churches, large or small, where there are visitors or strangers in the congregation the frequent attendance registration of all worshipers present is a "must." Members of the church should share in signing attendance cards, as requested by the minister, as an example to nonmembers to do so. One large downtown church averaged over 150 prospects each month for an entire year. Three-by-five cards for registering attendance may be secured from denominational sources in some cases, or like the card on the opposite page, may be inexpensively printed or duplicated in quantity for the particular church.

d) *A welcome or lookout committee*. In the church vestibule before and after services each Sunday they will secure scores of names and a great deal of useful information. After the service the ushers and the members of the congregation will willingly assist the welcome committee in extending their Christian greeting to strangers in the pews near them.

e) *Families and individuals* who have been served by the church and minister in baptisms, weddings, funerals, or counsel make up another source.

f) *Members of church organizations*. A careful checking of the membership records of the organized church groups, such as the men's club, the women's guild, the choir, the Girl Scout and Boy Scout troops, and others, will yield many additional prospects.

g) *Friends of church members*. From his circle of friends and acquaintances every member of any church anywhere can select one whom he could assist in bringing into the Christian fellowship. These names can be secured either by the minister in his routine calling in the homes of his parish, or by a letter to each member with the request that the name of any prospective member be sent to the minister on an enclosed postcard, similar to the one below.

*h) New residents in the community.* Many church members as an act of Christian neighborliness voluntarily call on any newcomer who moves into any residence near by, passing the name and any useful information on to the minister. In larger cities a rich mine of new residents' names can be secured or purchased from the "Welcome Wagon," the credit bureau, the gas or electric company and the *Legal News* or its equivalent, which often prints the list of those leaving the city or arriving as supplied by trucking companies.

*i) A guest book* in the vestibule and *guest cards* in the pew pockets will add many names to the prospect list.

*j) A friendly community study or census survey,* as described in step 3, may be conducted.

From these ten sources every church should be able

---

A PROSPECTIVE MEMBER FOR OUR CHURCH

Dear Pastor:

This person or family might become interested in our church.

NAME *Mr. and Mrs. Henry James*

ADDRESS *326 Monroe Avenue*

BUSINESS *Office, American Steel Co.*

You { may / may not } mention my name.

*Andrew Hopkins*
*Phone: Baker 3952*

to compile a master list of prospective members equal to more than one third of its total church membership. The clerical preparation of this master list, using cards like the one below, is a simple secretarial task.

**3. Conduct a census with the other local churches,** if one has not been held within three years. Such a project will create favorable comment, strengthen the ties of interchurch fellowship, discover the names of hundreds of unchurched adults and young people as well as scores of children for the church school. One Baptist church now has an overcrowded church school as a result of a survey that extended only four city blocks from the church. Training folders and census cards suitable for use in an interchurch friendly community study may be secured by an interfaith group or a ministerial association from the headquarters of any of the leading communions. Such a study should be made only if the churches participating are determined faithfully to call on all prospects discovered during the census. It is a

---

## Prospect and Assignment Card

Name *Roscoe M. Thornton – also Martha R.*

Address *905 Jackson Street*

REASONS FOR BEING ON OUR RESPONSIBILITY LIST

| | |
|---|---|
| _____ Member of Sunday School | _____ Attends Church Service |
| _____ Child in Sunday School | _____ Wife or Children Members |
| _____ Baby on Cradle Roll | _____ Attends Some Women's Meetings |
| ___X___ Survey—Prefer Our Church | _____ Attends Young People's Society |
| _____ Member Elsewhere | _____ Contributor |

Other Reasons or Information *Fairly new here.*
*Two small children should be in Sunday school.*

Called on by *W. K. Prince and W. E. Box* Date *March 21*

Report and Follow-up Recommendations *Secured commitment for profession and membership.*
*Pastor – please visit – preferably at night.*

grievous sin of omission to raise the hopes of the un-churched and then to disappoint them by failure to follow through with a membership call.

**4. Prepare a schedule for the crusade,** whether it is held in the autumn, during the Lenten season, or in both periods as many more thousands of churches are doing each year. An increasingly uniform plan of procedure and dates by the various denominations, whether the crusade is an interchurch community-wide effort or is conducted by a single church, includes the following features:

The friendly community study to be completed six weeks before the opening of the crusade

The preparation of the prospect list to be compiled four weeks in advance

The selection and enlistment of the workers three weeks before the crusade is launched

Announcement to the congregation two weeks in advance

All crusade plans completed one week before the crusade begins

The launching of the crusade on Sunday

The training and report meetings to be held on

SUNDAY     3:00 P.M.
           Why Evangelism Is So Important
           The Delightful People We Shall Meet
           How to Secure a Church Letter
           How to Secure a Commitment to Christ
MONDAY     6:15-7:05 P.M. Supper, reports, and instruction
           How to Visit Effectively
TUESDAY    6:15-7:05 P.M. Supper, reports, and instruction
           How to Win the Whole Family
           How to Handle Difficult Family Problems

WEDNESDAY 6:15-7:05 P.M. Supper, reports, and instruction
> How to Win Young People
> How to Assimilate New Members
> How to Form a Permanent Fellowship
> of Evangelism

Period of visiting and counseling by the minister, of those who have made commitments

Ingathering Sunday

**5. Choose your ablest members as workers.** The great task of evangelism deserves the services of the best people of any church. These representative Christians should be selected from the trustees, elders, officials, church-school teachers, and officers of such units as the women's organization and the youth group.

While few laymen could possess all the desirable qualities that would enter into the spiritual and mental make-up of the perfect evangelistic visitor, workers chosen should have many of the following qualifications: personality, superior intelligence and ability, tact, high standing in the community, personal religion, friendliness, loyalty to the church, devotion to Christ, and a willingness to attend the training conferences. Most ministers prefer to have the visitor list composed of about 75 per cent men and 25 per cent women, with one or two teams of young people. Others choose teams composed entirely of men; while still others secure excellent results from using couples, a husband and wife forming a team. The number of teams needed in any crusade will be determined by the number of names on the prospect list and the number of individuals or families each team is asked to visit. Experience indicates that if fifteen workers are selected for every hundred prospects, each team will have not more than ten or twelve calls to make.

Church-school teachers, leading young people, and outstanding women among the officers of the women's group are excellent workers because of their strategic position, ability, and influence in winning their friends to Christ and his church.

In addition to these specially selected visitors the minister should invite and urge every member of the church to endeavor to win some friend during the crusade. Evangelism is the high duty of every member and every organization of the church. One need not be a member of the evangelistic committee to share in the evangelistic task. Devoted laymen by the thousands speak the good word for Christ and his church among their acquaintances, associates, and friends. One Methodist layman, by setting aside an evening each week for evangelistic calling, won seventy-six new converts or members for his church in a single year.

**6. Enlist these workers personally.** The experience of thousands of churches proves that there is only one effective way of securing the ablest workers for the crusade. The minister must personally interview them and persuade them to share in this highly important task. He cannot delegate this duty to anyone else except under extreme circumstances; it is his most crucial single job in the campaign. He who uses the telephone or the mail will discover that he can enlist about one third of them; while he who clearly, enthusiastically, and urgently places the duty and opportunity of visitation evangelism before them in person will be successful in persuading about 95 per cent of them. Ministers have found the following presentation, which is in outline form only, highly effective as they have made their enlistment calls in home or office:

I have personally chosen you and nineteen other leading members from the entire membership of our church to do a kingdom task that is supremely important. You are admirably fitted to do it; and after I explain it to you, I am sure you will be glad to share in it. . . .

We have on the prospect list of our church the names of more than 120 families or individuals who are not yet members of our church. Some of them are parents of our church-school children, while others belong to our adult or young people's classes. Many of them have frequently attended our church services. A few are newcomers in our community. A large number of them are members of churches in other places and need only to be asked to bring their membership to our church. I am confident that we can easily win more than half of them. The membership committee, who worked out the plans for this visitation evangelism crusade, join with me in asking you to serve on one of the ten teams. . . .

The simplicity and definiteness of these plans will strongly appeal to you. Three weeks from next Sunday we shall launch the crusade, as many of the other churches of our community and our denomination are doing across America. At three o'clock that afternoon you and the other nineteen visitors will gather at the church for a training conference of instruction and fellowship. Then on Monday evening at six fifteen we shall all come to the church for supper, and at five minutes after seven we shall go out to visit the several families whose names I shall personally assign to each team. We shall return on Tuesday at the same hour for supper, reports, further instruction, and additional assignments for that evening, repeating this on Wednesday. No team or couple will have more than a total of ten or twelve calls to complete, which means about three or four an evening. . . . Already some of your friends—Mr. and Mrs. Simons, Mr. Paddock, Mr. and Mrs. Snider, Mr. Smith, and others—have gladly promised to do their share in this great work. I know you will want to take your place with them in this labor of love for Christ and your church. We shall all have a glorious time together. You will meet interesting people, enlarge the circle of your acquaintance, and with your teammate have the high joy of winning some of those on whom you call. I am sure, as your pastor, that I can count on you to do this for Christ and your church.

When the situation is presented in this or some better manner, refusals are rare except for the most valid reasons. Workers will readily record their promise on a card such as the sample visitation agreement above.

**7. Arrange for supper training conferences.** The supper meetings play an important role in the unfolding success of crusade in fellowship, training, and morale. Let the meal be simple but appetizing, served at cost by the women of the church or paid for out of the church budget. Let the meeting begin exactly on time and close on schedule. Let the spirit of the hour be optimistic and rich in enthusiastic fellowship in a great cause. The agenda for the conference usually follows this timetable:

6:00 P.M. Reports to the pastor of calls made by each team; assignment of calls for the evening

6:15 P.M. Supper, with one-minute verbal reports from three or four teams that have been most successful

6:40 P.M. Instruction period

7:00 P.M. Questions

7:05 P.M. Adjournment, with all teams on their way to their first call at once

**8. Assign graded prospect cards to visitors.** A valuable aid in assigning prospect cards wisely is to classify them according to the following code:

"A" stands for the best prospects, who are most easily won, such as the young people and children in the church school, people who want to transfer membership, parents of church-school pupils, and younger married couples.

"B" indicates that the prospect is good or fair, and that more effort may be required in winning him.

"C" is the least promising group, who should be assigned toward the end of the crusade after the workers have acquired more confidence and skill.

"S" is the code mark to be placed on the cards of that small special group of extraordinary leading people of the community, whose names should be assigned only to the strongest teams.

The assignment of prospect cards to the correct team can be done only by the pastor who knows best the age, interests, cultural level, and occupation of both prospects and visitors. The geographical assignment of cards should be used only as a last resort when more important factors and relations are unknown. Not more than six prospect cards should be placed in the envelope given each team as its first assignment at the close of the Sunday-afternoon training conference. On an average evening each team will hold about three interviews, the other three prospect cards being a reserve to take the place of any who are not found at home. The remaining calls each team will make during the crusade will be handed them at the rate of two or three each evening as they make their reports before supper. A careful record will, of course, be kept of the teams to whom prospects are assigned.

**9. Follow up with a program of assimilation,** as outlined in Chapter 7.

**10. Organize a year-round fellowship of evangelism,** if your church does not already have its equivalent. Under such names as "The Fellowship of Evangelism," "The Fisherman's Club," "The Evangelistic Club," and "The Evangelistic Fellowship," a permanent group of evangelistic workers can become one of the most valuable and delightful organizations in any church. They admirably supplement the intensive crusade effort with week-by-week or month-by-month evangelistic calling. On the crest of the tide of enthusiasm created by the crusade pastors find it easy to secure unanimous approval for the forming of a permanent fellowship to carry on this great work. They know that the joy they have experienced in winning someone to Christ and his church will be theirs again and again as they bring men to Christ and Christ to men across the coming months.

The weekly or monthly "order of business," under the guidance of the elected chairman and the pastor, usually includes, among others, the following features:

1. Prayers by four or five members of the fellowship.

2. Reports on the several calls made by each team.

3. Discussion and suggestions concerning the problems met in these calls.

4. Additional evangelistic training by the pastor with discussion.

5. Distribution of assignments for the next calling period.

6. Deciding the date and place of the next meeting of the fellowship—if possible, at the home of some member of the fellowship on invitation.

7. Light refreshments.

Any church anywhere that plans a visitation crusade carefully, energizes it with faith and prayer, and thoroughly cultivates its list of prospects with trained workers will reap one of the richest evangelistic harvests it has ever known.

# CHAPTER 4

# How to Train Laymen
# to Do Evangelistic Calling

## BASIC PRINCIPLES

1. The chief aim of every call is to secure a definite commitment to Christ and his church.
2. Instruction and training are indispensable to effective calling.
3. Valid appeals, persuasively presented, will secure about fifty per cent of favorable decisions on the first call.
4. All workers should be present at all the training conferences for instruction, inspiration, and reports.
5. The minister must act as leader, instructor, and inspirer of the entire crusade.

CHRIST displayed singular wisdom and sound strategy in choosing laymen—the Twelve and the Seventy—in instructing them in the good news of the kingdom, in kindling their confidence and enthusiasm, and in sending them out in teams of two to proclaim the kingdom and to serve the people. His worthy ministers today will follow his example and use his methods in spreading the good news of the kingdom and in meeting the religious needs of this modern age.

Each minister will desire to use much of the following training material, which in part is cast in the form of direct address, to supplement the training folders provided by his own denomination.

**Explain the purpose and importance of the crusade** at the opening of the first training period: "You have the honor and privilege of sharing in one of the most vital and important movements of our entire church year. You will represent Christ and our church in inviting those on whom you call to become Christians and to unite with our church. This is one of the finest services we can ever render Christ and the unchurched of our community. We shall all have his blessing, presence, and help as we undertake this task for him.

"Many of you are doing evangelistic calling for the first time. It is for you as well as for your fellow workers who have had experience that we hold these periods of training and instruction. Do your utmost to be present at every one of them, and at the end of the crusade you will be utterly amazed at how successful you have been. More than half of you as teams will win one or more people the first evening of your calling, while practically all of you will have secured from one to five or six decisions by the closing evening. Everyone will be grateful for your call, and I promise you that you will enjoy this work as much as anything you have done for your church in many years. And on Ingathering [or Membership] Sunday, which is three weeks from next Sunday, you will be justly proud to have had a part in bringing thirty or forty or fifty new Christians and members into your church.

"Visitation evangelism is not new: it is as old as the Christian religion. Jesus used it when he sent out his twelve disciples in teams of two to announce the good news of the kingdom of God. After their return he commissioned the Seventy—thirty-five teams of two each—

to spread the gospel more widely. Of this ancient, effective technique of securing converts Dr. Guy H. Black, who for many years has been an outstanding leader in the visitation evangelism movement, says, 'It is biblical, based on the New Testament and Christ centered; it motivates laymen and secures results.' Christ's disciples returned from their evangelistic crusade radiant with joy and thrilled with their success, *exactly as you will be before the end of this crusade.*"

**Describe the interesting types of prospects.** "In your calling you will find some of the finest and most interesting people you have ever met. Every visit will take on the spirit of an adventure in Christian friendship. You will find it fascinating and even exciting. All of your prospects, except a few discovered in the community study or census, have either attended our church services, or have children in our church school, or have in some way been served by our church. You will find the information concerning each on the prospect card. All of them need Christ and his church. They will gladly welcome you and will keenly appreciate your coming. Let me tell you of a few of them.

*Mr. and Mrs. Young-Family*, whose two lovely children attend our church school, and who will be easy to win

*Mr. and Mrs. Eager-to-Join*, who have just been waiting for someone to invite them into the membership of the church

*Miss Lonely*, who is hungry for the fellowship of a circle of congenial friends

*Mr. and Mrs. Out-Late-Saturday-Night*, who will offer you the excuse that they "just have to get their rest on Sunday so as to be ready for the work of the week"

*Mr. and Mrs. Sensitive*, whose delicate feelings were hurt by a "church member" thirteen years ago

*Mr. and Mrs. Fraternal-Order*, whose loyalty to their lodge

can never really take the place of their loyalty to Christ
and his church

Mr. and Mrs. Friendly
Mr. and Mrs. Newcomer
Mr. Argumentative
Mr. and Mrs. Sermon Taster
Mr. and Mrs. Loyal-to-the-Old-Home-Church
Mr. and Mrs. Newly-Wed
Mr. Night-Worker
Mr. Indifferent
Mr. and Mrs. Procrastination

You will be doing every one of your prospects a notable
service as you persuasively present Christ and your
church."

**Discuss the basic appeals to be used.** As an important part of his training every worker must become fa-
miliar with the chief general appeals, which create conviction and help persuade the prospect to make a favorable decision. The experience of thousands of churches
of all communions have found the following twelve considerations or appeals most effective.

1. *Christian belief.* When asked if he believes in
Christ and the Church, practically every prospect will
answer Yes. Millions count themselves as Christians who
have not yet united with any church. They need but to
be persuaded to translate their belief into action.

2. *Reason.* One's reason tells him that he should embrace and follow the highest. Jesus Christ is the divine-
human person who embodies the best. It is reasonable
and right to believe in, and to follow, him.

3. *Redemption.* When Christ is put at the center of
one's life, and thought and life are organized around
him, one's life is changed. Sin, fear, and selfishness are
driven out by faith, obedience, and Christlike living. He

shares with Paul that radiant experience expressed in the words, "I live; yet not I, but Christ liveth in me."

4. *Life.* The Christian way of living brings life at its highest and best. Faith in God and one's self, partnership with God in building his kingdom, power to achieve, courage to face the adventure of great living, adequacy to any situation, and the inspiring capacity for abundant living—all make one's daily life rich and wonderful.

5. *Conscience.* Every worker finds a powerful ally in the conscience of the prospect on whom he calls. "I know I ought to accept Christ and join the church," expresses the conscientious judgment of most thoughtful people. They know they should do God's will.

6. *The Christian home.* Good parents always desire the best in training, development of character, and friendship for their children. The Christian church provides the best religious and moral training in the community, while Christ is the one perfect example for both parents and children. No parent would willingly bring up children in a community where there was no church or church school. Every member of the family should find his place in the Christian fellowship.

7. *Fellowship.* A growing circle of good friends adds immeasurably to the enrichment of one's life. In these increasingly nomadic days one finds in the church, as nowhere else, the acquaintance and social fellowship one desires. Children and young people form wholesome friendships in the church, while adults forge ties of Christian fellowship that last across the years.

8. *A better world.* All people of good will would like to share in remaking the world according to a saner, sounder pattern. Christians, through their churches and through Christian missions, are in the vanguard of those who are creatively rebuilding the world. They plant

schools, churches, hospitals, clinics, and devoted Christian missionaries in non-Christian lands. There they become the heralds of a new age as they preach and practice the gospel of brotherhood, love, and the abundant life in Jesus Christ. Christians are the chief architects and builders of a better world.

9. *Service.* Every Christian and every church serves the community as well as the world in the name and spirit of Jesus Christ. Across the years a steady stream of inspiration, faith, courage, hope, integrity, service, and Christian character is poured into all the channels of community life. One is proud to share in this notable service.

10. *Influence.* The example one sets before those who know him is more potent than one realizes. Young people often walk in the footsteps of successful people whom they admire, while adults sometimes justify what they do by citing the practice of others. One's influence counts powerfully for the best when he is known as a Christlike Christian and a loyal church member.

11. *Duty.* There are few people who do not acknowledge some personal responsibility to God and to their neighbors. They are in part to blame for any evil conditions that can be found in their community. They recognize an obligation to help the Christian forces in their fight to make the neighborhood safe and wholesome for everyone. Parents realize that they ought to go to church and church school with their children instead of merely sending them.

12. *Personal friendship.* Prospects readily respond when the workers tell them that they asked to be assigned their names because of their personal friendship. "We have known each other for years," are the usual words of an experienced evangelistic visitor who has

won scores of his friends to Christ; "and I should have come over to talk to you about Christ and the church long ago. I ask you as your friend to accept Christ and to come into the fellowship of the church." One is touched and won far more easily by the appeal of a friend than he is at the invitation of a stranger.

From these twelve fundamental appeals the worker will select and adapt those he believes will be most effective in securing a commitment.

**Present Christ and the church positively.** Each worker present may be asked to state what he or she likes most about the spirit and program of the church. "What do you evangelistic workers like most about your church? What features of its spirit and work make it a desirable church home for those on whom you call? That we may have before us the chief phases of our church's program of service as talking points, I am asking each one of you to name one or two things about our church that please and help you most." Among the usual replies given will be the following:

The friendliness of our church
The sermons of our minister
The music of our choir
The spirit of reverence and worship in our services
The excellent Christian education provided for my children
  in the church school
The friendship and social life my son and daughter enjoy
  in the youth meetings
The world-wide missionary program of our church
The service rendered the poor and needy of our community
Our minister's activities in community and civic organizations
The program of our women's group
The help I get from the services each Sunday
The Bible study of the midweek service

The influence for good which our church exercises in the community

The friendliness of our church suppers

The opportunities to meet people through the men's club

The high standing of our church in the community

The comfort and help that come in time of sickness and bereavement

After the minister has added any important features that have been overlooked, he may say, "All of these words of commendation of your church come out of your own experience. You know them to be true. You have every right to be proud of your church and to urge all prospects who are or will become Christians to join it."

Each worker can then be asked to tell simply what Christ means to him. This brief period of Christian witness by the workers themselves is extremely important. It gives them confidence and experience in expressing what Christ means to them. It helps them clarify what he has done for them as they share with others their faith in him. One Presbyterian minister two or three days before the first training conference asked three or four of the more devoted Christians to be ready with their testimony in order that this part of the instruction period would move forward without delay. He said, "To each one of us Jesus Christ has brought more of inspiration, redemption, example, challenge, comfort, and help than can be expressed. Through him we gain the power for more abundant Christian living. I should like to have each one of you tell us in your own words just what Christ means to you." Among the usual words of witness will be the following:

Christ is to me my ideal and example for daily living

Christ is my friend and daily companion

Christ is my Saviour who keeps me from fear, sin, and dis-
    couragement
He stands by me as my helper in the hours of my deepest
    need
He gives me courage and strength
He makes God real to me
He gives me the spirit I need for meeting life successfully
He is the supreme teacher who shows me how to live

Then you can suggest to the workers ways of expressing
what it means to be a Christian. "Perhaps the simplest
and clearest statement of what it means to make a commitment to Christ is found in the catechism from which
I want to quote freely in this part of our training."

To be a Christian means to love and to trust, to obey,
and to follow, the Lord Jesus Christ. . . . Any child that loves
and obeys his parents can also love and obey Jesus Christ,
our Saviour. . . . Any young person who accepts Christ's
challenge "Follow me," can become a Christian. . . . Any
adult can become a Christian to whom "believing in the
Lord Jesus Christ" means "to accept him wholeheartedly,
and obediently to follow him as leader, friend and Saviour."
. . . Even an evil, sinful person who repents of, and forsakes,
his sins can become a Christian, for "God will forgive our
sins, cleanse our hearts from evil, and give us his holy
spirit." . . . Some of the normal requirements of the Christian life are obedience to parents and to conscience, prayer
and worship, love of what is good, right habits, the study
of Christian truths, and service to others. . . . Being a Christian does not mean that one immediately becomes perfect,
but rather it means that he has become a follower and pupil
of Jesus Christ.

Workers should be able to show the prospect how to
become a Christian. In a brilliant article in the *Chris-*

*tian* Advocate Dr. E. Stanley Jones, who has led hundreds of thousands into a rich fellowship with Christ, has listed six steps which the convert takes in coming into the fellowship of God through Jesus Christ.

1. I need Him.
2. I want Him.
3. I decide for Him.
4. I surrender to Him.
5. I will obey Him.
6. I will share Him.[1]

Commitments that might otherwise be vague and indefinite come clearly into focus as one sees the pathway by which he comes to Christ.

Christ and the church should always be presented in positive, winsome terms. "Your spirit in every call you make will be friendly and confident. The presence of Christ goes with you, while the spirit of God is already working with you in the heart of each prospect. Be natural. Persuade; never argue, since no one up to this time ever won a religious argument. Commend your Christ and your church with all enthusiasm and conviction. Be persistent without being irritating. Show tact and good taste, meeting objections and explaining matters that are not clear. Expect success. Have faith to believe that God will crown your best efforts with fine achievement."

Ingathering Sunday may be featured as the climax of the crusade. Focusing the attention of both worker and prospect on this day is sound psychology and good evangelism. The morale of the visitors is height-

[1] Pamphlet reprints of the article may be secured from *Tidings*, 1908 Grand Avenue, Nashville 4, Tennessee.

ened as they look forward to the harvest of their efforts, when those they have won are received into the church. Prospective members more easily give their consent when they realize that a large number of converts and members are to be received. One highly successful layman uses persuasive words such as these:

Ingathering Sunday will be for you one of the great days in your Christian life. You will remember it as the day you were welcomed into one of the finest, friendliest churches anywhere. With the large number who expect to join, you will feel that you really "belong"; you will have a church home.

**Explain how to secure members by transfer.** "Among your prospect cards you will find a number of people who were active church members in the communities from which they came. It will be your important and delightful task to persuade them to give their consent to have their membership transferred to our church. If you guide the conversation with tact and skill, as I know you will, the decision to transfer one's membership will not be difficult to secure, as there already exists a background of Christian obligation and church interest.

"First discover the name of the church and city in which your prospect lived. Then encourage him to talk about his former church home—his interests there and the services he may have rendered. Assure him that he will find in our church the same friendly Christian fellowship and opportunity to serve. Among the considerations and appeals you will find successful are these:

One should always have his membership in some church in the community where he lives. . . . One always feels so much more at home in a community, if his membership is in some church. . . . One's religious life and interests grow when one belongs to the Christian fellowship, while they tend to deteriorate if one remains outside the church. . . . One is worth ever so much more for Christ and his church as a member than as a nonmember. . . . Even though you plan to live here but a year or so, you will want that year to count for Christ and your Christian life. If you should move elsewhere, we would want you to transfer your church membership there. . . . We are sure you will find in our church the same kind of good friends who meant so much to you in your old church home.

"These and other appeals which you will make will help you in answering these two excuses sometimes offered: 'I want to leave my church membership in my old home church'; and, 'I am not sure how long I shall live here.'

"When you sense that your prospect's attitude is favorable, you may make your direct request in some such words as these:

Our pastor will be more than glad to write your minister telling him that you are now living in our community, and that you desire your church membership transferred to our church so that you may have a church home while you reside here. Your minister will be glad to send it, as our pastor is when any of our church members move to other cities. We feel sure that you will like to do this by signing this request card after you have filled in the name of your church and former residence. And it will be an honor and pleasure for us to take your request to our minister.

"God will richly bless you as you now receive your assignment and go out to make your first call."

# Chapter 5

# How to Make an Evangelistic Call

## Basic Principles

1. Evangelistic workers should always call in teams of two.
2. Prayer and faith vastly increase one's evangelistic effectiveness.
3. A friendly atmosphere and environment are important to efficient visiting.
4. A whole family can usually be won as easily as can an individual.
5. Most excuses and objections can be dissolved by tactful, friendly guidance.
6. The team must always visit until a frame of mind favorable to decision has been created.
7. Success will be proportionate to the training, ability, and experience of the workers.

A KEEN insurance man, who writes policies that total more than one million dollars a year, related to a group of his fellow church officials the open secret of the method that brought him success.

I first get all the facts I can about my prospect, his work, his probable salary, his home, the number of his children, and his resources. Then I decide what appeals or leads would be most effective in causing him to invest in insurance. I next explain to him the benefits and blessings of being well

70

insured and discuss with him how he can pay the annual premium. I tactfully set about persuading him that the best interests of his family and his future indicate that he should buy more insurance. Last of all, when he is convinced, I suggest that he sign the application. And after he has done so, I cordially thank him. I use these same principles of sound salesmanship when I commend Christ and our church to the prospects on whom I call.

Bringing Christ to men and men to Christ through visitation evangelism follows a technique strikingly similar to that used by Jesus and by those who would further any good cause. The comprehensive pattern includes the greeting of one's prospect, the introduction of the subject, the getting of the facts, the stating of the case, the answering of questions, the resolving of difficulties, the extending of the invitation, the making of the decision or commitment, and the closing of the interview. The following methods and suggestions for making an evangelistic call embody many of the most successful techniques used by thousands of churches of most communions in all parts of the United States. They are here phrased in direct address as examples, but the wise pastor will generously supplement them by drawing on the helpful and instructional material found in the training folders published by his own denomination.

**Make a favorable impression immediately.** You visitors will find that you will practically always be cordially welcomed by your prospect as he answers the door if you introduce yourselves in a natural, friendly manner with words such as these:

Good evening, Mr. Jones. I am Mr. Stewart, and this is my friend, Mr. Merwin. We are one of the teams of visitors from First Church. At the request of our pastor we came to make you and your family a friendly call.

If Mr. Jones does not instantly invite you in, use the information recorded on the prospect and assignment card by saying:

Your son and daughter, I believe, are in our youth group.
Your children attend our church school.
You have, I believe, attended our church services.

If the Joneses have company, or if you sense that they are about to go out, gracefully excuse yourselves with a promise that you will call again in a day or so.

Because first impressions are often lasting, you will wish to make the most favorable one possible at the beginning of your visit. Appreciate the children, the attractiveness of the home, and anything of special interest that you may note. Converse to discover such matters as the length of residence, the place of employment, and the names of any mutual friends. If any other members of the family are at home, suggest that they be invited into the circle, as you desire to visit with them also. If the radio is on, smilingly ask if it might be turned down or off while you talk with them about the important purpose of your visit.

The purpose of your call can be stated in words like these:

Our church is holding its visitation evangelism crusade this week, during which we laymen call on all those in any way connected with our church to talk with them about the church and the Christian life. Eighteen of us laymen are making three or four calls each evening, and we are glad to have been assigned your card.

The religious background of your prospect can easily be discovered. By asking a few simple questions you can find out your prospect's church connection, Christian background, and personal attitude.

You probably were a member of the church where you formerly lived? . . . You must have had many good friends in your old home church, did you not? . . . In what part of its work were you especially interested? Tell us about it for we should like to know.

Encourage your prospect to talk. If he was not a member of the church he attended, find out his present religious status through questions like these:

You doubtless attended the church school and church services where you formerly lived? . . . Do you count yourself as a Christian, one who believes in, and follows, Jesus Christ as his Lord and Saviour? . . . Have you been baptized, either as a child or later?

When you ask questions like these in friendly, Christian conversation, your prospect will willingly answer them. Share with him your own experience as he answers your questions.

You should aim to win all members of the family. You will be both surprised and delighted to find that it is as easy to win a whole family as it is to secure a decision from one person. The decisions of one or two members of the family will greatly influence all the rest. Having ascertained the interest and background of each, you will first aim to secure the decision of the one who, in your judgment, can be most easily won. This will probably be the mother or father, whose membership should be transferred to our church. Proceed to the other members of the family in the order of the probability of their commitment, building, of course, on the favorable decisions already made. In talking with you and children of appropriate age about becoming Christians, you will wish to adapt or grade your appeal.[1] The appeal to "complete the family circle" for Christ and his church is indeed a powerful one.

In the case of a Protestant–Roman Catholic mixed marriage you will find your task far easier than you might expect. Experience has proved that approximately one third of the Roman Catholics who contract mixed marriages can be won on the first interview, and that through cultivation another third will become converts. You will persuasively point out these facts: When a Roman Catholic has broken with his church and no longer attends, he is still a Christian in his soul. Tens of thousands of Roman Catholics are received into Protestant churches every year. Both Protestant and Roman Catholic are Christians. They worship the same God, who is the Heavenly Father of all. They believe in, and follow, the same Christ, who is the divine Saviour, and expect to go to the same heaven. The Roman Catholic Church is only one of the scores of Christian churches, such as the Greek Catholic, Presbyterian, or Baptist churches, all of which taken together make up the "holy catholic" or universal, world-wide Christian Church. Jesus Christ is the heart and center of our Christian faith. The Bible and our Christian consciences are our guides in Christian living. There is a radiant joy and a freedom from all fear in our Christian faith. You can present any other considerations you wish. You will find that the Roman Catholic will readily admit that he should attend some

[1] See Chapter 6.

church regularly, and that he can be persuaded to worship in our church with his family.

**State persuasively the reasons for becoming a Chris-
tian.** Millions of people in America are nominal, baptized Christians, who have not yet openly confessed
Christ or united with any Christian church. You will be
able splendidly to perform the delicate tasks of securing
decisions from them after you have had training and
some experience. You can almost always assume that
your prospect believes in God, that he admires Jesus
Christ and the Christian way of life, that he has probably attended a church school sometime somewhere, and
that he has a hope and expectation that he will sometime become a Christian and unite with a church. Since
you have so much in common with your prospect, share
with him the fact that you have been a Christian for
many years, that you have been deeply grateful for all
that Christ and the Christian faith have meant to you
across these years, and that in the church you have found
God, inspiration, courage for living life at its best, many
opportunities for Christian service, and a host of wonderful Christian friends. Tell him that you have come
to invite him to become an active Christian in the fine
fellowship of our church.

In addition to using any of the basic appeals which we
discussed at our last conference, you will find these
statements helpfully persuasive:

You do believe in God as your Heavenly Father. . . . You
also believe in Christ as the one you ought to follow as
Lord and Master. . . . You have doubtless often felt in your
conscience that you should become an active Christian. . . .
You wish your home to be Christian and your children
Christians, and you want your own example and influence

to count on Christ's side. . . . You probably believe, as I do, that the Christian faith is more needed today than ever before in our lifetime. . . . You would agree that God wants each one of us to live up to the highest and best he knows, which is Jesus Christ. . . . You have likely said that sometime you would become a confessing Christian, accepting and following Christ as your Lord and Saviour as faithfully as you can. . . . I believe you will agree with me that there is really no good reason for postponing your decisions any longer, and that this evening is as good a time as you will ever find to make your commitment to Christ and to begin your Christian life.

After your prospect has made his Christian decision, or if he is a member of a church elsewhere, you will wish to point his mind toward membership in the church by using any of the following appeals which you feel will be effective.

You no doubt feel, as I do, that it is the duty of every Christian to belong to some church. . . . You believe in the church and in its Christlike work here in our community and around the world. . . . Your own example and influence for Christ will be far stronger as a member of the church. . . . You will be more active and useful to Christ as a church member than you could possibly be if you did not belong. . . . You would not live in a community where there was no church. . . . If none of us Christians belonged to the church, there would be no churches. . . . Our church is doing a glorious work in Christ's name, and you want to have a part in it. . . . Christ wants us all to be loyal members of some church. . . . You could not choose a better or more appropriate time than Ingathering Sunday, when large numbers will be received into the church as the climax of this visitation crusade.

**Meet frankly all excuses and objections.** You should assume that your prospect is sincere, however flimsy and weak his excuses or reasons may be. Because he may honestly believe them, they should be dealt with fairly and fully. Encourage him to express himself freely in order that you may gain all the facts. You can easily distinguish between the alibis, the excuses, and the reasons. "I live far from the church and have no means of transportation" is a reason. "We are often out of town on Sunday," is an alibi. "I am so tired on Sunday morning that I have to get my rest" is an excuse. Most of these can be readily dissolved by tactful, friendly guidance. There is usually, however, one crucial factor that, like a key log in a log jam, delays or blocks a favorable decision. Discover this, and you are well on the road to success. Do your utmost to dissolve it without arguing or spending an undue amount of time on it. State winsomely your own judgment concerning the problem, remembering always that your personal witness is a potent solvent for objections and difficulties.

You should be prepared to answer these twenty common objections and excuses.

1. *"I am not sure how long I am going to live here."* If you are definitely planning to move soon, it will be wise to leave your membership where it is until you settle in your new home. If your plans are indefinite, and you may be here one, two, or three years, then by all means you should transfer your membership here. It should be where you live, and you may live here several years. Our church has provided a simple method of transfer. Our minster will be very happy to write for it; and if you move to another community, he will be glad to forward it there.

2. *"I want to keep my church membership in my old home church."* Your home church played an important role

in your religious life at one time, and I am glad to hear you speak of it with esteem and affection. Your membership there, however, is doing no good, while probably it costs the church something in assessments because you leave it there. Since you do not expect to return, and since you expect to live here, your affiliation should be where you are. An absentee membership usually becomes a dead letter, soon forgotten and easily lost. If nobody transferred his membership, all churches, including your home church, would in time have to close their doors, and none of us would want that.

3. *"We always send our children to church school."* You are doing a part of your Christian duty toward your lovely children in sending them regularly to our Sunday school. Don't you feel, however, that you are neglecting the rest of your duty to them, as well as to yourselves, by not going with them? You are right in feeling that good religious training is indispensable to their character and ideals. While they are small you can require them to go; but when they become thirteen or fourteen years of age, your example will be more influential than anything you can say. You would be willing to do almost anything to insure their physical health; come with them for the sake of the Christian welfare of your whole family.

4. *"There are too many hypocrites in the churches; I don't like some people who go there."* There are imperfect people in the church as there are in every lodge, club, or association. Christians are not perfect people but rather are going "on to perfection." No one remains out of a social group because there are hypocrites in it. You have a personal responsibility to God that is your very own. You should never permit a few imperfect folks to keep you out of the fellowship of God's people. To be really consistent you should join the church to set an example to help improve those who are not sincere. [The wrong answer to this excuse is, "Come on in, brother; there's always room for one more," however appropriate such a comment might be.]

5. *"I'm just as good as many people in the church."* It is extremely difficult to judge the goodness or badness of anyone, for under the same circumstances we might have done no better. The Bible says that we "all have sinned, and come short of the glory of God"; and "Judge not, that ye be not judged." You, however, are too big a man to compare yourself with some rather imperfect people. Christ is the one by whom we should measure our lives. When we do, he challenges us to measure up to the highest and to work with the best. I'm sure you would like to do that and as a Christian to come into our fellowship.

6. *"I do things of which the Church does not approve; I would have to give them up."* Whatever it is that stands between you and God, whether it be sin or evil or wrongdoing, should be given up whether you join the church or not. Your conscience and the Church ask you to give up only those things that are harming you or hurting someone else. By your decision to surrender them, and by your commitment to Jesus Christ as your Lord and Saviour, you can put them all out of your life. Through faith and prayer you can lead a victorious Christian life. God will give you joy, peace, happiness, power, and a score of other blessings worth infinitely more than the things renounced.

7. *"I'll do it sometime, but not now."* We are glad that you have determined that you will sometime become a Christian and unite with the Church. You have taken the first step in promising yourself that you will do what God wants you to do about your commitment to Christ—sometime. Is there really any reason why you should not make your decision now—this evening? If there is, I'll be glad to help you with it. If you think you ought to wait until you "know more about Christ" or are "good enough," you'll have to wait a long, long time. Accepting Christ will help you know him better and will aid you in living a more Christlike life. Your decision is an act of your will—a promise you make to Jesus Christ that you will be a Christian. That doesn't take long—just a moment. You have probably post-

poned this decision for a long time, and it has done no good to put it off. "Now is the accepted time." You should become a Christian this very evening!

8. *"I was compelled to go to church when I was young."* I was too, and I have always been deeply grateful to my parents for requiring me to do so. We were compelled to go to school, to learn to work, to keep clean, and to do a dozen other necessary things that we considered extremely burdensome at the time. One needs God at every age as his religion expands with his growing life. On the foundation laid in your boyhood you can build a strong faith and a rich life through Christ and the Church. In the old days services were too long and sermons too dull. I'm sure you will greatly enjoy and be helped by those we have in our church now.

9. *"I'll join when my husband [wife] does."* The ideal situation, of course, is where you and your wife unite with the church the same time. You worship together, and the spirit of your home is Christian. [Where the refusal to join on the part of husband or wife has extended across the years, it becomes the clear duty of the one who desires to unite with the church to do so. Each one owes a personal obligation to God, which one must discharge regardless of the refusal of anyone else. Often such an individual commitment causes others in the family circle to make a favorable decision.]

10. *"I can't believe everything the Church teaches."* Probably no two Christians in our church would completely agree concerning the meaning and importance of all the beliefs of the Christian Church. Perhaps my teammate or I can explain the one or two beliefs that are perplexing you. If we cannot, our pastor can. You do believe in the great fundamental truths of our Christian faith, and that is really the important thing. You will find that as you worship with us, enjoy the sermons, and share in the class discussions, these things will be much clearer to you. You remember when Jesus called his disciples, he did not ask them about their theological beliefs. He said only, "Follow me"; and

as they did, so they understood. That will be your experience too, I am sure.

11. "*I can't give to the church what I should like to.*" None of us can. Each one of us pledges "according to his ability," and that is all God wishes us to do. Give to the church only what you think God would have you give. The largest contribution you can make it, not your money, but your life. You can give that, and God will prosper you so richly that other things will care for themselves.

12. "*I don't like the preacher.*" We who work with Dr. Smith, and who know him well, feel that he is a devoted, hardworking minister who does his best to serve his church. In a church the size of ours we of course cannot secure the greatest preacher in America. We do have one who does his best, and we laymen do our utmost to help him. I'm sure you will like him, as we do, when you come to know him. One does not join the preacher, you know, but rather the Church. Ministers come and go, but the Church goes on forever.

13. "*I work so hard during the week that I have to rest on Sunday.*" Our service is set late in the morning for folks just like you, instead of at six, seven, or eight o'clock as the Roman Catholics do. Even though one stays up until twelve or one o'clock, he is still able to get a good eight hours sleep and get to church in ample time. We all have Sunday afternoon and evening in which to relax. I find that coming to church every Sunday refreshes and strengthens me. It is a tonic to my mind and spirit, and I always leave the service with renewed personal power. I'm sure God will give this to you also as you worship each Sunday with us.

14. "*I have just become careless and got out of the habit.*" That is one of the bad habits that all of us sometimes are tempted to form. Sickness comes, or we are out of the city, while we faithfully promise ourselves that next Sunday we shall, without fail, be in church. When we are absent, we disappoint God and our fellow members. When we are present, God richly blesses us as we begin the week. Every-

Sunday church attendance as a matter of conscience and duty is a must in every Christian's schedule. God gives us 168 hours in every week, and we all can surely set aside one for worship.

15. *"I live so far from the church and have no means of transportation."* That is a difficult problem, but perhaps we can help you find a way to solve it. If you have a car and drive it, you might agree with the other members of the family that you are always to have it late Sunday morning. It may be that one of our families living near you would sometimes bring you. Even though it would be impossible for you to attend every Sunday, you should still be a Christian and a member of Christ's Church, attending every Sunday that you possibly can.

16. *"I want to think it over; I'll decide later."* [This excuse is often a device for dismissing you or for entirely evading the question. Do not be misled by it, but return to the question of a decision by using words such as these, which have been found highly effective:] I appreciate your willingness to give the matter further consideration, but isn't it already clear what you should do? It becomes harder every time you put off the decision; no question is settled until it is settled right. You will have to face it again unless you settle it today; there is no easier or better time than now, and you will be glad you have made your decision.

17. *"I have tried being a Christian once and failed."* No Christian ever becomes perfect the moment he makes his decision to follow Christ. His acceptance of Christ is only the beginning of a lifelong pilgrimage toward perfection. Old habits and patterns of thought and action must be replaced by new, Christian ones. All Christians sometimes fail, but with God's help they try again and again and again. You must try again with faith that this time you will succeed. We believe you will and shall help you all we possibly can.

18. *"I'm out of the city so often on Sunday."* While we should like to have you with us in our services every Sun-

day, you could, as a Christian, worship in some church in the community where you are. Most loyal Christians make it a point of conscience to worship in some church on Sunday, wherever they are. You could do this, could you not? Then you could be with us in your own church the rest of the time.

19. "When I go to church, no one speaks to me." While that is often true of other organizations, I am extremely sorry that it happens in our church. I apologize for it. Sometimes we are so eager to see our close friends that we fail to speak to the strangers. I invite you now to come and sit with me next Sunday so that I may introduce you to a number of my friends. When you become a member of our church, you will feel much more at home. You will join one of our church-school classes, where so much of the social life of the church is carried on, and will yourself begin greeting the strangers who worship near you.

20. "I have a physical disability that keeps me from church." [This is probably the most difficult of all church attendance problems. Deafness can often be partially relieved if the person occupies a pew near the front of the church, where the music will not seem a confused roar of sounds and the minister's voice a faint, faraway echo. The installation of hearing aids has been found helpful by thousands of churches. Nervousness, which is often heightened to the point of distress when one is in a crowd, can be somewhat alleviated if the person sits in the rear of the church. Spinal conditions, which make it impossible for one to sit in one place for any length of time, make church attendance almost impossible. Such unfortunate people need Christ and the church even though they are prevented from regular attendance by conditions beyond their control.]

**Return always to your prime objective—a decision.** Your supreme purpose as an evangelistic visitor is, not to make a social visit, or to make a friendly call, or to win an argument, or to invite your prospect to attend church, but rather to secure a definite Christian decision *to follow Christ and to join the church.* After securing information, discussing a question, or dissolving an excuse you should return to the supreme objective of your visit. Your chances of success are far better on your first interview than at any other time. Guide the conversation so that it returns to the heart of the matter.

You can make it easy to say Yes and hard to say No. As Christ's lay evangelist you will do your utmost to avoid receiving "No" or "Some other time" as an answer. Frame your questions so that "Yes" will be the natural and logical answer. Instead of asking "Will you accept Christ?" persuasively frame your question:

You do feel that you should accept Christ, don't you? . . . You would like to do this now, wouldn't you?

By conversation you can change the thinking of your prospect from the negative to the positive. Continue to talk with him until you feel that his attitude is such that he will make the right decision.

You can often sense the favorable "psychological moment" for the decision. Because the winning of one admirably paves the way for the winning of all in the family, you will first secure the decision of that member of the family most easily won. You will then place one of the "Record of Commitment" cards in his hands, as you say,

I have here for you one of our decision cards, on which you may record your decision to follow Christ. You note the first line reads, "I believe in Jesus Christ and purpose with His help to live a Christian life." That is what you wish to do, isn't it? The next lines you see read, "I desire to unite with the ———— Church, and plan to present myself for membership Sunday," which is Palm Sunday, three weeks from next Sunday. That is your wish, also, isn't it? Then [here you will hand your pen or pencil to the prospect] you will wish to record your decision, as all are doing, by checking the statements on the card and signing it. My teammate and I shall be proud to present your commitment card to our minister.

If your prospect hesitates to sign it, talk further about the decision, and about how reasonable and wise it is to make it at this time. If he tries to return it to you, try gracefully to avoid taking it. Endeavor to discover what is preventing the favorable decision, and do your utmost to remove it.

You should not give up too easily. The habit of postponement and refusal may have become such a well-worn pattern in the mind of your prospect that he will seek to evade the issue. If he does, you will need to be patient, persistent, and persuasive. You have the right and duty, in a Christian way, to urge him to make the

---

### Record of Commitment

✓ I believe in Jesus Christ and purpose with His help to live a Christian life.

✓ I desire to unite with the _____First_____ Church, and plan to present myself for membership on Sunday, _____April 10_____

_____ I wish to transfer my membership to this church. For certificate write to _____ at _____

My name is recorded there as _____

NAME _____Roscoe M. Thornton_____

Address _____Martha Ross Thornton_____
_____905 Jackson Street_____

decision his conscience tells him God wants him to make. Strive steadily toward the goal of your visit, and do not permit yourself to be diverted from it by excuses or evasions. A few more minutes of conversation and witness may bring a convert to Christ and his church. After you have secured the first decision in the family circle, proceed with the other prospects in their proper order, using always the additional help of the one whom you have already won.

**Close the interview with a word of prayer.** When the decision has been made and the decision card signed, express your satisfaction and happiness in words something like these:

You have done just what God wanted you to do. You will always be glad that you made the right decision. This will begin a new period in your life, the happiest and most prosperous you have ever known. I should like to thank our Heavenly Father in a brief prayer.

Then simply and fervently thank God for the decisions, ask his richest blessings for the home, pledge faithfulness and love to Christ and his church, and claim Christ's presence and guidance with them always. Assure them of your pleasure and delight at being privileged to place their cards in the hands of your minister. Promise them that he will call in a few days to explain to them more about the Christian life, the privilege of church membership, Ingathering Sunday, and how they are to be received into the fellowship of the church.

The length of your call should be limited to about twenty-five minutes. Because few people are ever won after the first half-hour, you workers will wish to make the average length of each call approximately twenty-five minutes. By keeping close to the main purpose of your call, you will be able to complete it in this time so that you may go on to the other prospects assigned to you each evening. If your prospect happens to be one of the close-minded one-in-ten, or if the decision is clearly unfavorable and you can make no further progress, close the interview, leaving the card and asking the prospect to pray about the matter and to do what God would have him do. You can do this gracefully by saying,

We hope you will change your mind and make a favorable decision after you have prayed about the matter. Now you will excuse us as we have two or three other calls yet to make this evening.

By tactfully leaving your prospect in this manner you pave the way for another call, either by yourselves or by some other workers.

Christ will amazingly bless you as you do this great work in his name.

CHAPTER 6

# How to Win Church-School Children and Young People

## BASIC PRINCIPLES

1. The evangelization and training of children and young people are the chief hope for the future of any Christian church.

2. Christian commitment to Jesus Christ as divine Lord and Saviour grows best in the fertile soil of Christian education and fellowship through the church school.

3. Children and youth when winsomely challenged eagerly accept Christ and his way of life.

4. The act of commitment to Jesus Christ, whether made in the home or in the church, should be of supreme importance.

5. Church-school teachers, in co-operation with parents and the minister, are of immense help in guiding their class members to Christian decisions.

6. Converts and new members must be adequately trained before being received into the church.

AND the child grew, and waxed strong in spirit, filled with wisdom: and the grace of God was upon him. . . . And he said unto them, How is it that ye sought me? wist ye not that I must be about my Father's business? . . . And Jesus increased in wisdom and stature, and in favor with God and man." (Luke 2:40, 49, 52.) All friends of childhood and youth fervently wish that all children and young people might enjoy a Christian training as thorough and careful as was the religious training which shaped Jesus' growth as a boy in Nazareth. The Sabbath services in the synagogue, with the reading of the Prophets, deepened Christ's consciousness of the presence of God. The synagogue school, taught by that unknown rabbi-teacher, helped develop Christ's growing mind and heightened his understanding of the will of God. His religious home, chiefly perhaps through the influence of his mother and the disciplines of his trade, helped him develop a well-rounded personality which won the merited favor of God and man. Worship, education, and commitment are inseparably united in the childhood and youth of him who is the Saviour of mankind.

**Educate toward an early Christian decision.** Christian education and evangelism have an essential unity in personal religious growth. Christian education and Christian evangelism resemble the Siamese twins in that they cannot be separated without grave harm to both. They richly supplement each other in the service of the growing soul. A definite commitment to Christ and to the Church is the logical fulfillment and chief single achievement of Christian education. The Methodist Board of Education has stated the matter accurately and admirably in these words: "The supreme purpose of every Christian teacher is to bring each pupil face to face with God, with Jesus Christ, and with a major commitment to Him as Lord and Saviour." A definite process of education and personal growth precedes and follows the decision in any evangelism among children and youth that would be at its very best. What God hath joined together in the Christianization of young life, let no man put asunder!

The church-school class provides as ideal a setting for effective evangelism as is to be found anywhere in the church. The teaching ministry of the church school lays a firm foundation in knowledge for an intelligent Christian decision. Through graded lessons, study, and discussion the prospective convert comes to know the Christian message and the Christlike way of life. In the fellowship of the class group he comes under Christian influences, forms Christian friendships, develops Christian habits of thought and action, and shares in Christian service. The individual religious pattern is broadened and enriched by the group experience; and teaching, worship, service, and fellowship make almost inevitable a favorable Christian decision.

The most important, creative decision which a child of proper age, or a young person, can make is his first conscious commitment to Jesus Christ. Among all the other decisions and recommitments he may make as a Christian across the years, this one is supreme. It opens a new era of abundant living. It is the act of dedicating his life to the Master of men. It integrates his personality and unites his life with Jesus Christ. It sets before him the only perfect Example and Guide. It offers Christian ideals and standards of daily conduct. It gives his sense of partnership with God a vivid reality. It makes him a partner with Christ in bringing in the kingdom of God.

There are several chief objectives of evangelistic teaching. Any worthy teacher who would teach for a decision, instruct with a purpose, or teach for a verdict will adopt among others these important objectives of educational evangelism:

To lay a broad foundation for a growing knowledge of God as our Heavenly Father.

To present the life, teachings, and spirit of Jesus

Christ as the Son of God and the Saviour of the world.

To persuade all members of the class to admire, love, and follow Jesus as their example and guide.

To win every member of the group to Christ and to his Church.

To help new Christians to become more Christlike in their thoughts, actions, and attitudes.

To bring all unreached children and youth into the fellowship of the church-school class.

To challenge class members to share their time, talents, and money, that the world may become Christian.

To prepare all class members for those new decisions and additional commitments that are a part of every growing Christian life across the years.

An early Christian decision is extremely important. The fact that girls and boys today develop more rapidly than in former years and are more self-reliant and mature gives valid support to the practice of nearly all communions of lowering the age for Christian decision and confirmation. One denomination, which formerly set twelve as the necessary age, now administers the first Communion to children at the age of seven. Jesus made his decision to "be about my Father's business" when he was about twelve years of age. Most ministers and educators believe that—taking into the consideration that past religious training, home background, and the mental level of each child—the years between nine or ten and fourteen rank as the most reasonable and propitious for commitment to Jesus Christ. Thought patterns, religious attitudes, moral standards, and life decisions are often determined before, as well as during, one's teens. The importance of these formative, plastic years cannot be overestimated.

Children and young people are naturally religious.

Fortunately the dark days when original sin and infant damnation in their cruder forms were a part of the preaching and teaching have passed. In place of these hard theological tenets modern Christians put the teachings of Jesus, who held that every child is a child of God, that he is the object of God's love, that his soul is of infinite worth, and that each, through his growing faith in Jesus, can become progressively Christlike. Young people think and feel far more deeply about religion than their offhand, sometimes flippant defense mechanisms lead their elders to believe. Most of them at heart deeply desire what William James called "conversion"—"the process, gradual or sudden, by which a self hitherto divided, and consciously wrong, inferior, and unhappy becomes unified and consciously right, superior, and happy, in consequence of its firmer hold upon religious realities." They rise superbly to the challenge of what they believe is great and good.

**Evaluate child and youth evangelistic movements.** Whatever may be rightly said about the theological deficiencies and psychological shortcomings of certain evangelistic movements among children and young people, they evoke in an unprejudiced mind a generous amount of admiration for their keen strategy, their practical imagination, and their deep concern for the Christian welfare of the unreached. The movements' resourcefulness and devotion are a challenge and a stimulus to the conventional methods of the average church. About most of them there is a desperate urgency to get children "saved." They hold that children are lost until they confess their sins and accept the salvation Christ brings them through his Cross. The personal appeal is strong, with the accent on decision for Christ sometimes on the first or second day the child is in the class. The educational content is usually extremely limited, the chief emphasis being on confession of sins, faith in Christ, and decision for him.

One of the most promising and effective denominational movements for the evangelizing of girls and boys is that of the Northern Baptist Church, entitled "Winning the Children for Christ." Their plan includes "neighborhood bible-story hours," to which are invited all girls and boys from eight to thirteen years of age who are unreached and untouched by any church school. These gather weekly in a Christian home at a given hour on a set day through a five-weeks period under the guidance of a trained leader appointed by the local Baptist church. The program and curriculum include "songs, colored pictures, build-up pictures, and hand work, as well as stories and Bible memory work to interest the children in the gospel." Having learned something about Christ and his teachings, each child is urged to become a member of some church school, with the expectation that when he is prepared through further study he will accept Christ as his Lord and Saviour. The home of each child is visited by the leader, who seeks to arouse the interest and enlist the co-operation of parents. The possibilities of this program of service and recruiting seem quite unlimited.

That young people in large numbers can become deeply interested in vital religion has been repeatedly proved by both denominational and interdenominational youth evangelism movements. Whether they gather on Saturday night in some central hall or on Sunday night in the parlors of their church, they eagerly respond to a faith that is vital and real. They can be reached for Christ in great numbers, as is proved by the gathering of more than seventy thousand young people at Soldier

Field in Chicago, the more than ten thousand Methodist young people who met in Cleveland's great auditorium, and the scores of youth meetings held in the universities and high schools of America under the sponsorship of the University Christian Mission.

With such modern techniques as clever advertising, human interest stories, and the radio to announce their gatherings, these Christian young people—when not too severely handicapped by the conventional ideas of their elders—use humor, informality, lighting effects, musical instruments such as the xylophone and the saxophone, and laughter in the framework of their services. Although unconventional and sometimes almost spectacular, these features of the service work with the grain of the tastes and interests of many young people.

The heart of the service usually consists of witnessing to what Christ has done for those who give their testimonies, challenging everyone present to the acceptance of Jesus Christ as Lord and Saviour, or to reconsecration to him, and appeal for definite decisions for Christ and the Christian way of life. Contributing greatly to the spirit and results of the meeting are the happy singing of great hymns and the creative freshness of earnest prayer.

Though less vivid and spectacular than the mass-meeting appeal, the growing evangelistic movement within the youth organizations of the several denominations, wherein young people talk with and win other young people for Christ, is probably more far-reaching and permanent. Out of such church youth groups as the Christian Endeavor, the Westminster Fellowship, and the Youth Fellowship have come such splendid evangelistic movements as "The New Friends for Christ's Program" of the Northern Baptist Church, "The New Life for Youth Plan" of the Presbyterian Church, and

"The Youth Caravan" method of the Methodist Youth Fellowship. Through all these effective techniques of current youth evangelism, lives are changed, decisions are made for Christ and his church, commitments to Christian life service number into the thousands, and the radiant life of the Son of God touches young life with glorious promise.

**Enlist teachers as evangelistic leaders.** "Every Teacher an Evangelist," which was the slogan of the National Christian Teaching Mission, represents the evangelistic ideal in securing from children and youth a whole-hearted commitment to Jesus Christ as Lord and Saviour. Being in a position of favored privilege and duty, the teacher spends a hundred times as much time on the average with his pupils as does the minister. He leads them in religious teaching and discussion. He supervises their unfolding religious life and knows better than anyone except their parents the Christian needs of their growing personalities. He enjoys their confidence and close friendship as he worships, thinks, studies, and plays with them. Who better than he can help them lay upon the altar of surrender and sacrifice their Christian decisions?

The wise minister will place upon the hearts and consciences of all church-school teachers their high evangelistic privilege. He will train them in the fine art of leading their class members to a definite decision at the proper time. He will place in their hands booklets and folders that will aid them in this God-given task. He will prepare a list of the prospects and nonchurch members of each class, placing this with decision cards in the hands of the teacher. The minister will invite their suggestions for making Decision Day or Recognition Day more impressive and meaningful. He will help each teacher with any problems or difficult cases. He will aid them in every possible way in bringing those they teach into a living, loving fellowship with Jesus Christ.

**Secure the active co-operation of parents.** Because the family group should always be basic in both Christian education and evangelism, the teacher or the minister will plan to discuss with the parents the matter of their children's decisions and to enlist their consent and co-operation. While some teachers and pastors call on parents and secure the decision of children in the same visit, increasing numbers pay two visits, one to be assured of the parents' approval and the second to secure in the presence of their parents, the decisions of the children who are of proper age.

As able insurance men cleverly appeal to the better human emotions, such as the care of one's children and the provision for one's wife or husband in the event of death, so will the teacher or pastor persuasively present the case for Christian decision. In conversing with parents, tell them of the church and church-school plans for inviting girls and boys of proper age to accept Christ and to unite with the church. Point out that their son or daughter has arrived at the age when these commitments are usually made. Mention the fact that many others in the same class or department are making their decisions at this time. Indicate that across the past months and years their child's church-school training has been preparing him for this decision. Outline the plans for Decision Day. Describe the course of special training and instruction the child will receive in the membership training class during the coming months. Inquire concerning baptism, and offer to arrange for this service. Speak of the reception of converts and new church members on Ingathering Sunday. Make clear that further training across the coming years will prepare their child for his growing Christian life. Stress the desirability of an early Christian decision. Cordially invite and expect their wholehearted help. Arrange the time when you may return to talk with their son or daughter in their presence.

Where parents are not Christians or members of the church, they often can be easily won with their children to make their own Christian decision.

**Challenge young people to Christian commitment.** Because girls and boys are so easily persuaded to say Yes to those they trust, the guiding of them in their Christian commitment must be delicately handled if it is to be the creative, meaningful and wonderful experience God intended it to be.

One of the most practical and successful methods used in interviewing girls and boys is that employed by a young Methodist minister, the substance of whose appeal is as follows:

I have come over to talk with you and your parents, James, about accepting Jesus Christ and becoming a member of his church. It is the most wonderful and important thing anyone ever does, and I want to explain it to you. In your church and church-school class you have learned that God is your Heavenly Father, that he created this world for us, that he loves you, that he sent Jesus to earth that first Christmas Day to teach men how to live, that Jesus is our pattern and example, that he loved us so much that he gave his life for us, and that he wants each one of us to love and to follow him. You do love Jesus, don't you? You want always to be the kind of boy Jesus wants you to be, don't you? You would like to be like him. You do want to belong to him, to follow him, and to have him as your friend, don't you? This is what we call becoming a Christian and accepting Jesus as our Lord and Saviour. You would like to do this now, wouldn't you? Your mother and father are Christians and members of the church, and I know you would want to be like them. I'm talking also with the other members of your class, all of whom I feel sure will wish to accept Jesus and to unite with his church. That is what you would like to do now, isn't it? I have here a decision card that I want to read and explain to you. The first line reads "I believe in Jesus Christ and purpose with His help to live a Christian life." Since this is your wish, would you not like to sign your name to this decision card?

After the decision is made, you should explain the purpose and procedure of Decision Day if one is to be held. Indicate the time and place of the membership training class. Tell of the plan for confirmation or uniting with the church. Warmly congratulate the child on his decision. Offer an earnest prayer of gratitude and petition for God's blessing, guidance and care.

Young people respond with idealism and daring to the challenge to follow the young man Christ, whether presented by the teacher, the pastor, or one of the fellow members of their class. Most of them want to enlist in, and give themselves to, the great crusading causes in the world. With high courage they will embrace the kingdom of Christ when presented as the supreme cause that gathers up the best in all the world's worthy movements.

Young people by the thousands have already proved that when adequately trained and properly guided, they can win their friends in great numbers to Christ and to his church. With the help of their teachers and leaders they are bringing Christ to youth and youth to Christ. The Northern Baptist Church in its handbook *A Weekend of Youth Evangelism* has cleverly outlined the training and calling procedure under the following attractive heads:

THE 4 Do's
Gain an entrance into the home.
Secure a favorable environment.
Begin with your prospect where he is.
Come to the purpose of your visit.

THE 4 DON'TS
Don't do all the talking.
Don't argue.
Don't stay too long.
Don't become discouraged.

THE 4 BE's
Be natural.
Be enthusiastic.
Be persistent.
Be kind.

A large part of the instructions to visitation evangelism workers, found in Chapters 4 and 5, can easily be adapted to effective use by young people in their evangelistic training classes.

Leaders of youth often find that young people in their evangelistic calls break away from the conventional methods and use their own startling language and technique. The captain of a Texas basketball team, with his forward, called on the captain of another basketball team and said, "I would like for you to become a Christian." He then read him the first line of the commitment card, which ran, "I believe in Jesus Christ and purpose with His help to live a Christian life." He then continued: "We will let you sign this card if you will quit drinking, gambling, and running around, and will accept Jesus Christ and join the church and come regularly to our young people's meetings every Sunday night." They talked the matter through, and the other captain made his promise, registered his decision, and has been living a wholesome, growing Christian life ever since.

"Getting someone to decide for Christ is the most important thing in the world!" exclaimed a young woman who had won a number of her friends to Christ. "This is real," said a college young man who had found new meaning and challenge in life through his faith in Jesus Christ.

**Conduct an impressive Decision Day service.** When properly prepared, Decision Day—sometimes called Recognition Day or Declaration Day—can be an important event in the growing Christian life of children and young people. The public declaration of the decision, made in the presence of parents and recorded during the departmental worship service before fellow members and teachers, tends greatly to confirm and reinforce the commitment. Almost universal approval is accorded by pastors and teachers to these two principles: All group pressure or mass psychology should be avoided in the case of children who are unwilling or unready to make their decision; and all children of the proper age in the department must be interviewed and, if possible, won before Decision Day.

The minister will of course conduct the Decision Day service. He will confer with the departmental superintendents and the teachers in working out an appropriate order of service for the day. He will bring his Decision Day message in thoughts and words graded to the age group he addresses. His message will include, among other appeals, the privilege, duty, and joy of being a Christian, the call of Jesus for all to follow him, the challenge of living the Christian life, the blessings that flow from one's Christian commitment, and the invitation of those who will make the decision to come forward. He will invite the teachers to come and stand with the pupils they have helped win. He will confirm their decision in his prayer of dedication.

The continuing growth in Christian grace and knowledge after decision and reception into the Christian fellowship is a long and important process that requires and deserves the finest skills of teacher, parents, and pastor. Commitment is to be progressively completed in Christlike consecration to the will of God. Christian habits must be formed; Christian faith must be deepened; Christian stewardship must be practiced; Christian worship must be enjoyed; Christian education must be continued; Christian service must be expanded; and new decisions and commitments to the purposes and plans of God must be made across the years.

This harvest of evangelism and Christian education among children and young people is the most strategic and important of all the opportunities before the Christian Church.

# CHAPTER 7

# How to Build New Members into the Life of the Church

## BASIC PRINCIPLES

1. A Christian commitment must be followed by a process of Christian training, growth, and assimilation into the fellowship of the church.

2. Careful instruction in the life and teachings of Jesus, as well as in the history, beliefs, and program of the church, helps lay a firm foundation for permanent loyalty and intelligent churchmanship.

3. The formation of such Christian habits as daily prayer, Bible reading, church attendance, stewardship, and service is indispensable to continuous Christian growth.

4. Each new member should be assigned to a "fellowship friend," to some church-school class, and to other appropriate fellowship or interest groups.

5. Each new member should be encouraged to make a generous pledge to his church and to invest his talent and his time in its program of service.

6. The depth of the convert's Christian life and the permanence of his relation to the church will be largely determined by the thoroughness with which he is integrated into the Christian fellowship.

THOUSANDS of good ministers of Jesus Christ across America have transformed the appalling yearly losses in church membership into substantial net gains.

The open secret of their success is found in a thorough, intelligent program of assimilation. By using the finest spiritual tools and techniques, they build an extremely high percentage of their converts into the permanent fellowship of the Christian Church.

In all too many churches more time and effort are spent in getting a convert to join the church than in making sure that he remains in its fellowship as a growing Christian. Far too many ministers are clumsy workmen who woefully neglect, or tragically fumble and bungle, the religious life of the new Christians committed to their pastoral care. Heavy membership losses are made inevitable by such unchristian methods.

Personal Christian growth and church loyalty should be assured as the chief objectives in guiding the new Christian or church member in his new way of life. The decision to become a Christian is the beginning, not the end, of the Christian life. It is his enlistment in the army of the Lord, his commitment to Christ and his way of living. Training must follow enlistment, that he may grow in grace and in the knowledge of our Lord and Saviour, Jesus Christ. He will then go on to perfection in active Christian service and fellowship.

Most of the following features of the successful assimilation programs of large and small churches of many communions can be used by any church of any size anywhere.

**Give personal guidance to all new members.** The minister's spiritual-guidance visit to each new member before he is received ought always to be a creative Christian experience. The new Christian must have the friendly counsel of his minister and spiritual adviser. A new era of partnership with God is opening. Old habits must be broken and new ones formed. He will adopt

Christian patterns of thought and ideals. He will find new friends and form new convictions which are a part of any worthy Christian life.

This personal conference gives the minister a unique opportunity to do these things:

To confirm and deepen the decision already made.

To discover the religious background and need.

To counsel concerning unchristian practices and attitudes.

To explain what it means to be a Christian.

To state what is involved in being a church member.

To recommend a discipline for daily Christian living.

To make clear the obligation one takes when he joins the church.

To outline the plans for Ingathering Sunday.

To present the membership manual and to state the time and place of the membership class.

To establish a lasting bond of trust and friendship between the new member and his minister.

The minister should give guidance in forming these Christian habits. The dominant role of habit in forming Christian character is recognized by religious leaders everywhere. One learns by doing. He develops by acting according to the Christlike pattern. One talented Baptist minister counsels each convert or new member concerning religious habits in substantially these words:

As a Christian you have accepted Jesus Christ as your guide and example. You are eager to think and act and live as he would have you. He formed, among others, seven religious habits which you will want to make your own if you do not already have them.

*The practice of God's presence* is the first. God is always with you and near you in the invisible but real presence of Jesus Christ. Christ walks with you; he is the companion of your every way; he helps and strengthens you; he promises, "Lo, I am with you alway."

*Daily prayer* is another Christian privilege you will want to observe regularly. Prayer is more than asking God for gifts or begging his help in time of trouble. Prayer is fellowship and conversation with your Heavenly Father through Jesus Christ. It is friendship with the God whose presence you feel. Pray to him in the morning as you start the day, in the evening when you have finished your tasks, and as often through the busy hours of the day as you desire.

*The reading of God's Word, the Bible, daily* will bring you faith and courage. Through it he will speak to you his message for the day. In it you will discover how others, with his help, lived radiant, victorious lives.

*Every-Sabbath church attendance* follows another habit of Jesus, who always worshiped in the synagogue, "as his custom was." God and your minister expect you at church every Sunday unless you are ill or away from home. God gives you 168 hours during the week; he wants you as an absolute minimum to set one of those hours aside for worship in his house. The fellowship of God's people, the music of the hymns, the reading of the Scripture, and the inspiration of the sermon will help you immeasurably in your growing Christian life.

*Christian stewardship* is the name we give to the habit of sharing our time, our talent, and our income in the spirit of Christ. You undoubtedly have abilities, skills, and interests that will enable you to render a splendid service to your church. While I am never the financial agent of the church, I do encourage each new member to begin the practice of setting aside a definite portion of his income for God's world-wide work. Some of us are tithing stewards, which means we set aside ten per cent of what we earn for Christian work. It is wonderful to be in partnership with God in helping Christ build his kingdom on earth.

*Grace at meals* and the making of one's home life Christian will bring God's presence and blessing to those in your family circle. From the youngest to the oldest each can take his turn in giving God thanks for the good things all enjoy. I have brought for you a copy of the daily devotional booklet which our church publishes for the devotional use of all our families. You will find it a great help.

*The habit of faith* is the last of the seven important Christian habits that I urge you to form. Always expect the best of life. Believe that it holds for you richer gifts and greater victories than you have ever known. God is your active partner, and Christ is your comrade and helper. Live a life of eager, ardent, expectant faith, and you will be able to say with Paul, "I can do all things through Christ which strengtheneth me."

As your minister I am asking you to promise God and yourself that you will do your utmost to cultivate these seven Christian habits. You will make that promise, will you not? You may count on me to help you in every possible way.

It is as important as it is easy to discover, by guided conversation, the interests, abilities and experience of each new member. Some larger churches request each new member to fill out an "enlistment for Christian service folder" in which are listed the chief areas of church life in which his experience and interests might qualify him to serve.

Personally presenting each new member with the membership manual—a copy of the official catechism or prayer book of his communion—offers an opportunity to stress its continuing value. One successful pastor, in presenting the membership book to each new member before he joins, says in substance,

Our church always gives one of our interesting membership books to each new member before he is received.

This copy is yours as the gift of your church. In it you will find a record of the chief events of the life of Christ, with his teachings, the history of the Church across the centuries, and the beliefs and customs of our own church. The privileges and obligations of church membership are also listed, as is a great deal of other valuable religious information. As you read it carefully, you will find the answer to a great many of your questions. Later you may wish to lend it to friends who are prospective members for our church. If there are any matters about which you have questions, I shall be glad to answer them in our membership class. After you have been received, I shall fill out the certificate of baptism and of membership.

Increasing numbers of pastors place their pictures in the front of the membership manual and add a personal word of welcome.

**Train new members in a membership class.** The membership training class offers most communions in America their greatest unused opportunity to build Christian loyalty and sound churchmanship. The local church is the training camp where the Christian recruit receives instruction and training in the arts of his Christian warfare. When his training is thorough, he usually becomes a good soldier of Jesus Christ. When it is shoddy or inadequate, he is soon found to be A. W. O. L.

Some communions do a superb piece of instruction and indoctrination for their converts. The required period of study ranges from one to three years, with Christians transferring from other communions required to attend membership classes. In bitter contrast other churches and ministers give less instruction to their new members than would be necessary to join a Boy Scout troop.

The church school when adequately staffed with competent teachers does render invaluable service in laying a broad foundation for the intensive training of the membership class. Let every minister "take heed how he buildeth thereupon." The steady lengthening of the period of instruction for children, young people, and adults ranks among the important trends in American Protestantism.

**Receive new members impressively.** Whether they are welcomed before the entire congregation at the Sunday-morning service or by the officials of the session in the quiet friendliness of the church parlors, new members have the right to expect that their reception into the Christian fellowship will be a memorable occasion. The minister can make it an impressive, creative, life-changing experience or just another dull, perfunctory reading of a formal ritual.

It is a thrilling sight to see the girls and boys of the membership class, after careful instruction, pledge their love and loyalty to Christ and his church and then kneel for their confirmation or prayer of blessing. In many churches parents, church-school teachers, and godparents stand with them as they are received.

Adults also deeply appreciate the dignity and reverence shown by the minister in the service, as well as the warmhearted welcome by the congregation. In many churches they then sign the church register.

**Integrate new members into the church fellowship.** As soon as possible they should be introduced to the officials at an evening reception meeting of the session, official board, or congregation. They deeply appreciate the privilege of meeting the leaders of the church and their wives. Brief words of welcome by such officials as the superintendent of the church school, the president of the men's or women's group, the chairman of one of the important committees, and the president of the youth organization will acquaint new members with the spirit and program of the church. Their sense of strangeness fades; their circle of acquaintances grows; and they feel that they belong in their new church home. Some churches hold this meeting as an "orientation conference" *before* the new members are received.

Meeting neighboring members is even more important. All too often new members who have been besieged with invitations to join the church find themselves strangely neglected or ignored—except by the finance committee—after they have united with the church. The assignment of each new member's or family's name to three neighbors, living within a short distance, with the request that they call soon, will result in a broadened acquaintance and a growing friendliness as the circle of Christian fellowship widens.

Each new member should be assigned to the proper organization who will see that the root of religious interest finds nourishment in the rich soil of Christian fellowship and service. He should join a church-school class if he does not already belong. Young people are eager to share in the activities of the youth group, while men and women appreciate the friendly contact with their respective fellowships.

The appointment of a "fellowship friend" or sponsor for each new member is excellent strategy. Among his important duties are these:

To act as counselor and friend for the new member or family.

To make friendly calls at his home.

To sit with him at the church service and to introduce him to friends.

To make sure that he meets the teacher of the proper

church-school class and the leaders of appropriate church organizations.

To discover the reasons for any absence from the Sunday services.

To make certain that all members of the family are securely integrated into the active life of the church—generally, for a period of one year.

A personal invitation to a social or friendship evening at the parsonage, manse, or rectory will be highly prized and long remembered by all new members. Ministers find that this delightful affair forges added personal bonds between them and their new parishioners. Selected officials, with their wives, are glad to take their turns in entertaining each membership class. After an evening of fellowship, conversation, games, and refreshments each feels that his life has been enriched by a larger circle of Christian friends.

**See that new members fulfill their vows.** No time is so important as the first year of membership for forming right habits, and never is the member so ready to carry out his promises as he is immediately after making them. This is the time to call upon him for specific fulfillment rather than wait till he has become neglectful.

1. *Urge church attendance every Sunday* unless illness prevents it. It is the delicate and highly important task of the pastor and the fellowship friend to make sure that each new member acquires the holy habit of every-Sunday church attendance. In his spiritual guidance visit the pastor will have emphasized the duty and privilege of every Christian to worship in God's house on his day. He will have stressed this again in the membership training class as a sacred obligation.

The fellowship friend must carefully note the presence

or absence of the new member for whom he is responsible each Sunday. He will make a telephone call or pay a friendly visit to discover whether illness or absence from the city kept his new friend from church the previous Sunday. He will express the assurance that he expects to see him at the service next Sunday. Where the situation becomes too difficult for the fellowship friend to handle, he will, of course, notify his minister.

2. *Secure a pledge or contribution promptly.* Each new member stands ready to honor his promise to give financial support to the church in its growing program at home and abroad. No time is more propitious for securing a willing and generous pledge than the week after reception into church membership.

Many churches mail new members a package of contribution envelopes, together with a personal letter explaining the financial plans and needs of the church. This letter is followed in a few days with a friendly call by one of the members of the finance committee, who more fully describes the broad program of service, answers any questions, and secures the pledge. New members often form an unfavorable opinion of the management of any church that does not immediately indicate how a new member may make his expected contribution. Sharing through a pledge is a worthy expression of loyalty.

3. *Enlist his abilities and talents in the work of the church.* The minister, who asks each new member to promise that he will render some service to Christ and his church, is under obligation to help him find his place and task, if possible, somewhere in the broad program of activity. In many churches one official holds several positions, while far less than one third of the abilities of the total membership is geared to the work of the church. In their former church homes many new members

carried their full share of responsibility. When their talent has been discovered and enlisted as committee-men, evangelistic visitors, or associate teachers in the church school, the life of the church feels new strength.

4. *Ask him to win some friend for Christ and the church.* The churches of America may profitably consider the custom of the Christian church in Korea, which requires each new member, before he is admitted to full membership, to win some acquaintance or friend to the Christian life. Every convert has a number of friends, at least one of whom can be brought into the Christian fellowship. Each should be asked, both before and after his reception into membership, to take the definite responsibility for winning at least one friend during the year as a service of love and loyalty to Jesus Christ. Those qualified should be invited to serve with the fellowship of evangelism in the continuous evangelistic work of the year.

**Remember the membership anniversary.** New members warmly appreciate the thoughtfulness of their minister as he writes them a personal letter or makes them a friendly pastoral call approximately one year after they took their vows and were received into the church. Their first anniversary can be made an occasion of high promise and rich opportunity. Their loyalty and service can be commended if they have been faithful, while counsel and encouragement toward greater Christian achievement may be offered. If they have become indifferent or neglectful, they can be reclaimed for the kingdom and again vitally related to their church.

Handsome dividends across the years will accrue to any church and minister who will carefully and thoroughly build new members into their Christian fellowship.

# CHAPTER 8

# How to Launch a
# Church Loyalty Crusade

BASIC PRINCIPLES

1. Church attendance in any church anywhere can be increased 25 to 100 per cent.

2. The church services and sermons must first be improved before any church loyalty attendance crusade can be permanently beneficial.

3. The minister, as preacher and worship leader, largely determines the value and attractiveness of any service.

4. The religious needs of young people and children must be served directly or indirectly in each service.

5. Church-school members of all ages can be won in large numbers to regular church attendance.

6. October—beginning with World Communion Sunday—the New Year, and the Lenten season are the three best times for launching an attendance crusade.

7. A co-operative community-wide church attendance crusade will greatly strengthen the movement in each local church.

THE problem of getting more of the saints out of their homes and into their churches on Sunday morning and evening is one for which every good minister of Jesus Christ is seriously seeking a solution. Whether he preaches to a metropolitan congregation or serves a

113

rural parish, he wistfully wishes that the other two thirds of his church's members were present also as he leads his people in their worship.

If church attendance were an elective in the school of Christ, neither the minister nor the members would need to be greatly disturbed by the grave disparity between the total membership and the number of worshipers at a regular service. In primacy and importance, however, every-Sunday church attendance ranks with prayer as among the highest, holiest habits in a growing Christian life. Christ himself set the worthy example by going each Sabbath to the synagogue "as his custom was," while the writer of Hebrews warned against "forsaking the assembling of ourselves together." To the devout Roman Catholic, Sunday is a "day of obligation," and the failure to attend Mass is a sin. To the faithful Protestant Christian, every-Sunday worship at church is a spiritual privilege, a religious opportunity, and a Christian duty; and the failure to be present is a grievous sin of omission.

How can the absentee members be persuaded to return? How can these lost sheep who have strayed from the fold be reclaimed? How can these inactive Christians be reactivated? How can these indifferent Christians be rewon to a renewed loyalty to Christ and his church? Not by preaching alone, since the habitually inactive members are not present to hear the sermon. Not solely by pastoral calling, for the task is far too great for the minister alone. There is a highly effective way, and thousands of large and small churches of all communions across America have discovered and used it effectively. It is the church loyalty movement, a sustained effort by pastor and layman based on improved church services and implemented by the church attendance crusade.

All the leading denominations of the United States recognize the high wisdom and sound strategy of a steady, intensive effort to reinterest and reclaim inactive, indifferent, nonattending members of the church. Under such names as the "Church Loyalty Crusade," "Church Loyalty Visitation," "Fall Recovery Crusade," "Church-wide Loyalty Campaign," "Christ-centered Crusade," "Community-wide Church Attendance Crusade," "Lenten Loyalty Movement," and "See-You-in-Church-Sunday Crusade," they are encouraging and urging their churches to go to the people and to win them to a renewed loyalty to Christ and his church. The chief purposes of the movement include the following:

1. To strengthen the Christian loyalty of all members of the church.

2. To persuade inactive, indifferent members to return to church.

3. To spread the blessings of worship and preaching as widely as possible.

4. To cultivate the habit of every-Sunday church-attendance.

5. To lift the spiritual life of the church to higher levels.

Intensive church loyalty efforts usually center in one or more of the three periods of church-attendance opportunity offered by the Christian year. The one most widely observed opens with World Communion Sunday, the first Sunday in October, and continues either to the end of the month or to Thanksgiving Sunday. The second begins with the first Sunday of the New Year, when the church works with the seasonal urge of the New Year's resolution "to attend church every Sunday." The third cycle is that of Lent, Ash Wednesday through Easter, when the seven Sundays in Lent offer a unique opportunity for urging every-Sunday church attendance.

Phenomenal results have been achieved in such attendance crusades when they have wisely included improved services of worship, better preaching, and a faithful follow-up. One rural church increased 40 per cent, while a city congregation which usually numbered 200, rose to an average of 380. Another church required two services each Sunday for a period of eight months to accommodate the crowds; while a city church in New Jersey, by steady cultivation and pressure across three years, increased its church attendance more than 500 per cent. Every church that faithfully follows the crusade technique is definitely strengthened.

**Analyze and evaluate your church attendance.** Why do people come to church? A positive approach to the problems of absenteeism is the discovery of why people attend church at all. While the factors producing adequate motivation are often numerous and complex, the following twenty-six reasons from the lips of church attendants, representing types all the way from the faithful Christian to the peripatetic sermon taster, include the chief ones:

I formed the habit as a child.
I meet God and am blessed as I worship.
I always learn something from the minister's sermon.
I love the hymns and the other music.
The popularity and reputation of the preacher brings me.
I feel it my Christian duty.
I believe every parent should set the right example to his children.
The church helps me train my children in moral and religious matters, and I feel I should attend and support it.
Many of my friends attend.

I am always in church on Easter Day.

I always feel better after going to church.

The hour of the Sunday service is the most helpful and inspiring of the entire week.

Churches are necessary, and there would be no churches if all people refused to attend them.

I get there a sane, balanced perspective on life.

I find friendship and comradeship there.

The sermon subjects intrigue my imagination.

I like to hear the Bible read and explained.

I find that God does not prosper me if I do not attend his church.

I find help in living my life.

I gain help in discouragement, difficulty, and sorrow.

The Sacrament brings God near to me.

I like the minister and his sermons.

Church attendance increases my spiritual and moral resistance.

I find new courage to face life.

The standing and prestige of the church attracted me.

Only the church is taking Jesus Christ seriously.

Why are about two thirds of your church members absent on an average Sunday? Valid reasons and flimsy excuses are strangely mixed in this list of twenty explanations that have been seriously offered by members for their nonattendance:

The sermons are so poor and uninteresting.

I have just carelessly got out of the habit.

I got so far behind in my pledge that I stopped coming.

I live so far from the church and have no means of getting there.

Shabby auditoriums and shoddy services do not interest me.

I feel uncomfortable about attending church when I cannot give what I would like.

My church-school class is my church.

I'm so tired Sunday morning I just have to rest.

My parents compelled me to go to church when I was young.

I have no one with whom to leave my two little children, who are too young to come to Sunday school.

I can worship God in my own home by radio.

I do things the church doesn't approve of, and I feel uncomfortable when I attend.

Because of my long illness I just got out of the habit.

I didn't like the old minister, and I don't like this new one.

The noise of crying babies and whispering members spoils the service for me.

I'm just as good as some members who attend church regularly.

I'm waiting for my husband to attend with me.

Since my wife died, I feel utterly lost without her beside me in church.

My lodge is my church.

I have a physical handicap that keeps me from church.

Whatever may be said about the "dangerous ages" when members lose interest, such as adolescence, the college years, the marriage–young family period, and old age, many of the above answers reveal a tragic ignorance of the true nature of the Christian Church and a woeful lack of any deep conviction that regular church attendance is a binding Christian obligation.

A breakdown of the total attendance figure of his own church as counted rather than estimated will reveal a condition that will amaze and shock even the most careless minister. A simple "church-attendance analysis chart" such as the following will help present a true picture which, if not complimentary, will at least be honest and challenging.

1. Total membership of your church     _____
2. Number of worshipers present     _____

3. Nonmembers present       _____
   *a*) Children               _____
   *b*) Visitors               _____
4. Number of church members present   _____
5. Number of church members absent    _____
6. Proportionate number present—one in  _____

With the facts before him one minister bluntly asked himself pertinent questions like these:

What stress have I placed on the privilege and duty of every-Sunday church attendance?

Have I urged every-Sunday worship as a sacred Christian obligation?

Have I emphasized the values and benefits of regular attendance?

What efforts have I personally made to reclaim indifferent members?

Have I asked the leading laymen of my church to cooperate in this important work?

Have I led my people in a real church loyalty crusade?

To what extent am I personally responsible for the small attendance in my church?

**Plan improved church services and special sermons** that will deserve and hold larger congregations. A highly successful business executive once advised his assistant, "Always improve your product and make it more attractive before you launch your advertising campaign." The wise minister of Jesus Christ will improve his service of worship and preaching to a high level of excellence as an indispensable prelude to any church loyalty movement.

He was not a cynic who said that the average church service is about as well attended as it deserves to be. All too often the service fails to begin on time; worship is carelessly planned and clumsily handled; the solo is an example of amateur exhibitionism; the prayer is a prosy ritual or an extempore exhortation; the sermon is an unprepared procession of platitudes; while Christian fellowship and friendliness at the close of the service are all but extinct. One who failed to find in a Scotch church the inspiration and fellowship he longed for wrote these biting lines:

> As cauld a wind as ever blew,
> A cauld kirk, and in 't but few,
> As cauld a minister's ever spak—
> Ye'se a' be het or I come back!

It requires only candor to admit that frequently the worship of God is justifiably associated in the common mind with dullness, and the sacred services with the stuffy and stereotyped.

What are the primary purposes of a public service of worship and preaching? Gifted ministers and thoughtful laymen have answered in these words:

To make God real to men as a presence and an experience.
To be in touch with eternity for an hour.
To push back the horizons of the soul.
To interpret life religiously and sacramentally.
To renew the spirit of Christlikeness in the Christian.
To be rebuked, forgiven, and challenged to increasing Christlikeness.
To preach the gospel of the Son of God.
To recharge the batteries of the soul with divine power.

The minister, as preacher and worship leader, is responsible for the value and attractiveness of any service. If he treats divine realities flippantly or crudely, if his attitude is one of formal indifference or undue familiarity, if his sermons are timid or trite or tedious, and if he leads his people in their worship in a careless or slovenly manner, he must not be surprised if his small congregation fails to find the bread of life. If, however, he encourages his people to expect great things from God during the service, if he handles holy things with dignity and reverence, if he chooses great sermon themes and presents them with vigor and conviction, if he takes the great truths of the Bible and makes them adventurously alive in terms of everyday life, if he brings the best of his research and study to bear in solving the perplexing life situations of his hearers, and if he challenges youth and age to courageous faith and heroic living, then not only will he have a growing congregation; he will have brought God to men and men to God.

Make *worship* the experiencing of the presence and love of God.

Read the *Bible* as the Word of God.

Exalt the *sermon* as the message from God.

Offer *prayer* as communion with God.

Provide *music* that really glorifies God.

Let the *sacraments* bring the blessing of God.

**Utilize methods of attracting attendance** by appealing to special interests and needs. One of the most promising long-range trends in Protestantism is to be found in the increased provision for *children* in and during the church service. The church that cares for and serves her children in public worship will both win the good will of their parents and also cultivate the Christian habits of every-Sunday church attendance at that period in life when their minds are most impressionable. A nursery and kindergarten for the tiny children during the entire church service will enable parents to attend church, as well as the entire congregation to worship undisturbed.

Thousands of ministers encourage the boys and girls of the primary and junior departments to sit with their parents or church-school teachers during the first fifteen or twenty minutes of the regular service of worship. A three-minute children's sermon on some Bible story or religious theme brings their pastor's message to them in ideas and language that they can understand. While a hymn is sung, they pass out in their children's recessional to the expanded or third-period session of the church school, where during the remainder of the service they engage in hand work, visual education, the memorization of Bible passages and hymns, together with other phases of the religious educational program that will supplement the training they receive during their regular church-school hour. In this way they receive twice the religious instruction provided by the average church school.

Young people of high-school age and above represent another section of the community which in most church services are often conspicuous for their absence. Youth can be attracted and held to regular church attendance by any minister who intelligently includes them in his planning. A sermon to young people; the observance of Youth Sunday and Family Sunday; the participation of young people from time to time in the church service, through reading the Scripture, ushering, lifting the offering, and giving the prayer; and the preparation of every sermon with the needs and interests of young people in mind—all these have been found to challenge, attract, and hold young people to the church.

The church school can be of great help in cultivating church attendance among children and young people—and among adults. Fortunately the dark ages of division between church and church school, when each regarded the other as a competitor or a substitute, are rapidly passing into an era of cordial co-operation. They supplement each other in a rich unity—the church at church and at worship.

Church-school members of all appropriate ages can be won in large numbers to regular church attendance in these ways:

Provide for the preaching and sermonic needs of children and young people, as suggested earlier in this chapter.

Place emphasis on both church and church school—two glorious hours of worship, teaching, and preaching.

Announce from the pulpit the attractive features in the departments and classes of the church school.

Enlist the co-operation of each departmental superintendent and of the teacher and president of each adult class.

Request that a verbal or written announcement be made before each adult class, similar to this one:

"Our Glorious Christian Faith" will be the subject of Dr. Smith's sermon this morning at the church hour. All members of our class, including the visitors, are urged to remain for the service.

Observances of the *chief Sundays and special seasons* of the Christian year possess high value as church-attendance builders. Attractively planned and widely announced, they both lift the average attendance figure and can mark the beginning of a new loyalty to the church. Among these are the following:

RALLY DAY in September for members of the church,

church school, and youth groups after the vacation period.

WORLD COMMUNION SUNDAY, when Christians around the world share in the Sacrament of Holy Communion as their pledge of allegiance to Jesus Christ and as a symbol of their religious unity.

REFORMATION SUNDAY, which offers an opportunity to bear the Protestant Christian witness.

WORLD ORDER SUNDAY, when patriotic organizations can be invited to join with the Christian Church in laying the foundation for a just and durable peace.

THANKSGIVING SUNDAY, most American of all holidays, when all men should express their gratitude to God for his bounties and blessings.

CHRISTMAS SUNDAY, when through gladness, gifts, and good will, Christians observe the birthday of their Lord.

NEW YEAR'S SUNDAY, a day of dedication to renewed loyalty and spiritual planning.

LAYMEN'S SUNDAY, when an effort can be made to assure the attendance of all men in the membership and constituency.

THE SUNDAYS IN LENT, when the continuity of a series of sermons on the great truths of the Christian faith make every-Sunday church attendance an attractive duty.

PALM SUNDAY, with its accent on victorious Christian living.

EASTER DAY, with its glorious message of immortality.

MOTHER'S DAY, when faithful sons and daughters pay a special honor to their mothers.

PENTECOST SUNDAY, which has been called the "birthday of the Christian Church."

CHILDREN'S DAY or STUDENT'S DAY, when the church's interest in childhood or youth is featured.

*Christian friendliness* builds attendance. A friendly greeting by a layman with a cordial invitation to "come and worship with us every Sunday" acts as a powerful magnet in drawing visitors and strangers to the services on succeeding Sundays. Just fifty years ago a rather timid young man entered one of America's leading churches on the first Sunday after he had left home. He was greeted by a genial lawyer who sat near him and was introduced to two young men of his own age. He said recently, "I was desperately lonely that first Sunday in the city, but the cordial greeting from that friendly lawyer was responsible for my joining this church." One would have difficulty in finding more handsome dividends than those paid on this investment of a few minutes of one's time in friendliness and fellowship at the close of a church service.

The welcome committee, sometimes called the lookout or cordiality committee, assisted by the ushers, can render a notable service in increasing church attendance as they greet visitors and members before and after church. The friendly smile, the gracious greeting, the courteous seating of strangers, and the exercise of care and good taste in welcoming everyone will be factors in the drawing power of any church service.

**Outline the crusade campaign schedule.** The planning and launching of the church loyalty crusade to increase church attendance and to reclaim inactive members is in many regards strikingly similar to the procedure already outlined for the visitation evangelism crusade in Chapters 3, 4, and 5. As the minister makes his tentative preliminary plans:

1. He will secure from his own denominational headquarters samples of the cards, folders, and letters for the crusade and will then order an appropriate quantity for his church.

2. As chief leader, planner, inspirer, and conserver of

the crusade he will carefully think through the movement in all of its phases.

3. He will tentatively decide, and subject to the approval of the crusade committee, the time when the crusade should be held and the goal in church attendance that should be achieved. He will undoubtedly choose the month of October, beginning with World Communion Sunday, as one period. He may also include the New Year's or Lenten period for a second or third church-attendance effort during the year in order that his church may attain the goal of 50 or 60 per cent of its membership in attendance every Sunday.

Then the crusade schedule or timetable should be made up, using the autumn church loyalty crusade as an example. Pastors will find in the following crusade schedule, which includes the best features suggested by the various denominations, many helpful suggestions which they can adapt to the needs of their own local church.

FOURTH WEEK BEFORE CRUSADE OPENS

1. Select the crusade committee.
2. List the purposes and choose the goal of the crusade.
3. Set dates for the opening and closing of the crusade.
4. Select the ablest possible church loyalty visitors in numbers adequate to call on all the members of the church.
5. Plan the services and sermon subjects for the Sundays of the crusade featuring World Communion Sunday and other appropriate special days such as Family Sunday, Youth Sunday, and Guest Sunday.
6. Outline the announcements and publicity for the crusade.
7. Place the names and addresses of all families of the church on assignment cards.

THIRD WEEK BEFORE CRUSADE

1. Call on and enlist the church loyalty visitors.

2. Secure instruction folders or prepare a mimeographed outline of plans and instructions for the visitors' training conference.

## SECOND WEEK BEFORE CRUSADE

1. Announce the crusade at all Sunday services and in all classes and departments of the church school and the youth groups, giving full information concerning its purpose and program.
2. Divide the assignment cards into groups of five, seven, or ten, and carefully assign these to the appropriate visitor.
3. Write or phone all visitors reminding them of the day and hour of the training conference.
4. Hold the visitors' training conference for instruction and counsel.

## LAST WEEK BEFORE CRUSADE

1. Commend the crusade at all Sunday church gatherings, and urge complete co-operation and every-Sunday church attendance throughout the crusade.
2. Send out the church loyalty visitors on Sunday afternoon, with the request that they complete their calls by Wednesday, four days before World Communion Sunday.
3. Announce the church loyalty crusade in the local press, including the names of the crusade committee and the visitors.
4. Mail to the entire membership the World Communion letter, enclosing a communion card for each member of the church.

## FIRST SUNDAY OF CRUSADE—WORLD COMMUNION SUNDAY

1. Make the World Communion service a glorious Christian experience.
2. Commend the loyalty of all present, and claim for the church services their every-Sunday attendance.
3. Take the attendance registration through the com-

munion cards, which are to be dropped on the offering plate or left at the communion altar.

4. Announce any special features for the coming Sundays of the crusade.

FIRST WEEK OF CRUSADE

1. Follow up all absentees by phone, letter, or "We Miss You" card.

REMAINING WEEKS OF CRUSADE

1. Register church attendance, using attendance registration cards every Sunday.
2. Feature Family Sunday, Youth Sunday, and Guest Sunday in the most attractive manner possible.
3. Announce in pulpit and press the growing success of the crusade.
4. Arrange follow-up visits on inactive members by loyalty visitors and church officials.
5. Make pastoral calls on those who have declined or refused to attend.

**Enlist and instruct the crusade visitors.** The fine abilities of Christian laymen represent the greatest reservoir of unused power in any church. When these are geared to the task of persuading inactive members to every-Sunday church attendance, the results are amazing. In character and standing the visitors chosen should rank in the upper 25 per cent of the membership. In numbers they should total about 10 per cent of the membership of the church, so that as they go out in teams of two, each team will have from seven to twelve calls. When interviewed personally two or three weeks before Visitation Sunday, almost 100 per cent of those selected will agree to serve. Universal experience proves that a telephone call or a letter is an extremely poor substitute for a pastoral or personal interview.

One Presbyterian minister of a rapidly growing church uses persuasive words like these with the visitation agreement card:

We are planning a great church-attendance crusade this autumn for the purpose of securing every-Sunday church attendance by every member of our church. The committee and I have chosen you, with others from the entire membership of the church, to help in this important task. Your task will be to call with a teammate on from seven to ten families of our church to secure their promise to be present on World Communion Sunday and to attend church on the remaining Sundays of October. About fifty of us will meet two weeks from next Wednesday evening for instruction and training and shall make our calls the following Sunday. You will find this important work delightful and worth while, and I am sure you will be willing to serve for the sake of Christ and your church.

This pastor always secures almost 100 per cent of those he invites.

A visitors' training conference must be held for instruction and counsel. Increasing numbers of churches find that a supper meeting on a Wednesday evening before Visitation Sunday works with the grain of convenience and interest as a suitable time for giving training and instruction and for receiving assignments. Some churches make this supper a complimentary one. The program of the conference, under the guidance of the minister, will include:

A statement of the purposes of the crusade.
The presentation of the material contained in the denominational training folder.
The technique of making a loyalty call.

The method of discovering and dissolving objections and
of securing the signing of the loyalty card.

An instruction period for the workers.

The passing out of assignments for Visitation Sunday, with
an adequate number of "Church Loyalty Covenant" cards.

Closing with prayer for God's help in achieving the highest
success.

Visitation Sunday afternoon, either following dinner
at the church or at three o'clock, will open the church-
wide, every-member visitation effort, with all calls completed and all reports made at the church on Wednesday
evening.

**Register everyone present on crusade Sundays.**
The securing of the names of all worshipers present on
each Sunday of the church loyalty crusade is both important and necessary to the crusade's highest success.
The loyalty committee and pastor will thus more easily
and accurately discover the names of the absentees, who
for some reason failed to attend. The attendance registration feature, used in the church vestibule either before
the service or as a part of the service itself, causes the
congregation to take church attendance more seriously,
while the registration cards are a fertile source of the
names of new prospects for church membership. The
attendance card is placed in the hands of each worshiper
as he enters the church, or is clipped to the church bulletin, or is distributed during the church service, and is
later dropped on the offering plate, as described in Chapter 3. In smaller churches, where practically every church
attendant is known, a simple check of those present takes
the place of the attendance card.

The registration makes possible a needed follow-up.
Because it takes longer than one or two Sundays to
establish the habit of every-Sunday church attendance

in the lives of some members, it is necessary to re-call on those who have not attended church during the first two Sundays of the crusade. Ask one of the more successful workers to make another call in an attempt to rekindle interest and to secure a promise of regular attendance during the remainder of the crusade. Those difficult cases which fail to respond should receive a call from the minister, who as a result of his interview will decide what should be done in each situation.

Any church anywhere can greatly enlarge its every-Sunday congregation if it will make the intelligent and persistent effort to do so through a church loyalty movement.

# Chapter 9

# How to Win Inactive Members to a Renewed Loyalty

BASIC PRINCIPLES

1. Most of the inactive members of any church can be reclaimed to a recovered loyalty and to regular attendance.

2. The valid reasons for every-Sunday church attendance, when persuasively stated, will appeal to every member.

3. Representative lay members, after training, can persuade most of their inactive fellow members to attend church regularly.

4. The excuses and reasons for absenteeism must be discovered and dissolved.

5. A definite promise in the form of a signed decision is valuable in cultivating the habit of church attendance.

6. The most difficult cases must be cared for by the minister.

7. Members who show renewed interest must be assimilated into the fellowship and activities of the church.

THE reclaiming of inactive members to a renewed loyalty to Jesus Christ and the reassimilation of them into the active fellowship of the church are extremely important phases of any adequate program of evangelism.

132

These are the lost sheep who have gone astray into unchristian paths of religious indifference and even of moral and spiritual danger. They constitute a challenge to every church and minister and represent one of the major problems facing the Christian Church.

The fact that the majority of them can be rewon to the Christian way of living through a church loyalty crusade has been proved by the experience of thousands of churches. Teams of trained laymen, calling in the homes of absentee church members and talking with them about their duty to Christ and his church, have invariably had amazing success in re-establishing their inactive fellow members in their church. The technique of making an effective church loyalty call, which is the theme of this chapter, will be fully explained and discussed by the minister and workers at the workers' training conference. With the exception of the instructions in blackfaced type and the material in brackets, the following paragraphs are cast in the form of direct address, such as the pastor would use in his hour of instruction.

You are the chosen representatives of Christ and your church in one of the most important and interesting pieces of Christian service which you have ever rendered. The privilege and task which you and your teammates have will be to call on eight or ten of the families of our church to help them to a deeper loyalty to their church and to every-Sunday attendance at its services of worship. Every interview will be an adventure in Christian fellowship. You will enjoy this great work; and because of your devotion and training, you will, with God's help, be highly successful.

**Acquaint workers with types they will visit.** Let me first introduce you, in imagination, to some of your active and inactive fellow members on whom you may call. You will let me name them in terms of their church loyalty and attendance characteristics. Some of them are the most faithful Christians to be found anywhere, while others will need your counsel and help. Among them are:

*Mr. and Mrs. Loyal,* who deeply love their church and minister, and who, regardless of the weather, are always in church on Sunday

*Mr. and Mrs. Friendly,* who generously support the church, and who are present fairly regularly

*Mr. and Mrs. Active,* both of whom hold office in the church's organizations, and who are eager and willing to do anything asked of them

*Mr. and Mrs. Behind-in-Their-Pledge,* who have grown discouraged, and have dropped out of the church because of their unpaid financial obligation

*Mr. Bereaved,* who since his wife's passing feels utterly lonely when worshiping alone in church

*Mrs. Aged-and-Infirm,* whose physical disabilities keep her away from church

*Mr. and Mrs. Nobody-Speaks-to-Us,* who have not yet found in our church the warmth and friendliness that you have

*Mr. and Mrs. Tired-Sunday-Morning,* who are "just so weary" that they think they must sleep all Sunday morning

*Mr. and Mrs. Critical,* whose powers of faultfinding amount almost to sheer genius

*Mr. and Mrs. Worldly,* who have gradually acquired tastes and habits that make them uncomfortable, and even ashamed, in church

*Mr. Once-a-Year-on-Easter,* who as a chief "outstanding member" has never realized that there would be no church if all were like him

All of these fellow members will cordially welcome you. Most of them will gladly co-operate in the purposes of the crusade. Others will require your patience, persistence, and persuasion because of long-standing habits or prejudices. A few, perhaps one in ten, will require the guidance and counsel of your minister.

**Illustrate the approach for a church loyalty visit.** A great deal of common ground already exists on which you may stand with even the most indifferent fellow members of our church. In talking with any member, you should start with these seven valid assumptions, the foundation on which you may help him build a reactivated Christian life:

That he is, or was, a Christian.

That his name is on the church roll as a member.

That at one time he was interested and attended the church.

That he has often resolved to "begin again."

That he will at first offer excuses or reasons for his loss of interest and his absenteeism.

That he knows in his heart that he should be a more active Christian and churchman.

That he probably feels an obligation and a desire to renew his loyalty.

The following is one of several successful ways to open a visit. As your fellow member answers the door in response to your knock or ring, you will introduce yourselves in some simple, effective way such as the following:

Good afternoon [or good evening]. I am Mr. Johnson, one of your fellow members of our church, and this is my friend, Mr. McKnight. We are out making some friendly calls in this neighborhood on members of our church and had the good fortune to have your card assigned to us. If it is convenient, we should like to come in for a few minutes to tell you about our church loyalty crusade.

After other introductions have been made, and all are comfortably seated, use the next three or four minutes to establish a friendly atmosphere through conversation about matters of mutual interest, such as the home, the family, friends, the church, or the community. The weather has never been found too profitable a topic of conversation. Let your spirit always be that of friendliness and understanding, as the purpose of your call is "to win friends and influence people."

You could state the purpose of your call in words something like these:

As you doubtless know, our church is launching next Sunday her church loyalty crusade, which all of us believe will lift the life and service of our church to the highest levels in recent years. Its aims are a deeper loyalty on the part of all members, every-member church attendance every Sunday, and a stronger, better church. Our pastor has carefully planned the services and sermons for the month of October so that they may be the finest possible. He has chosen us and nineteen other teams of visitors to call on the entire membership of the church this week to invite and urge them to promise to do these three things as their part in the crusade:

First, to be present on World Communion Sunday, which is next Sunday, the opening of our crusade.

Second, to rededicate their lives to Christ, to their church, and to a more Christlike way of daily living.

Third, to attend church on each of the other three Sundays of the crusade during October, unless prevented by a personal illness or absence from the city.

As loyal members of our church, and as workers in the

crusade, we have made these promises ourselves. We are cordially inviting you as our fellow members to do the same.

Converse next about the good work the church is doing. You will wish to guide your visit toward the church and its growing program of service.

We are sure you believe with us that Christ and the church are more needed today than ever before. They represent the best hope we have for a better world. Our children sorely need the ideals and character building of our church schools to keep them from juvenile delinquency and to give them the finest in life. Our young people need the guidance and friendships which they find under the wholesome conditions in our church, while we who are older find the spiritual refreshment and inspiration which come to us through our fellowship with God and his people. Through our missionary giving we are reaching across the seas to bring brotherhood and to help rebuild this broken world. You and I have a right to be proud of the great and good work our church is doing.

Next you will state the case for every-Sunday church attendance. The reason for regular church attendance, when clearly and persuasively presented, will help create the conviction that every-Sunday worship is a Christian duty as well as a privilege. To help those you visit to understand this obligation more fully you will wish to use three or four of the following points, enlarging on them as you see fit:

1. Christ would have each one of us be present for worship in God's house every Sunday unless prevented by personal illness.

2. Every Christian owes God and himself one hour of worship in church out of the 168 hours of each week.

3. Every Christian every week needs the inspiration, confidence, faith, encouragement, and strength which he receives from God through the church service.

4. One's example to one's family and neighbors definitely influences them.

5. Every-Sunday church attendance is one of the finest and most helpful habits any Christian can have.

6. One's Christian life grows as he worships, while he loses something vital and valuable out of his life when he fails to meet with God and his people.

7. The educational and friendship values of the service and of the periods before and after the service are great, as one meets and greets his fellow members and friends.

8. If everyone attended church, the community would be far better than it is; while if everyone remained away from church, there would be no churches.

9. One meets God and receives his blessing more helpfully on Sunday at the hour of worship in church than anywhere else in the world.

10. God prospers those who are faithful to their church, spiritually and in other ways.

**Evaluate the real reasons for absenteeism.** About one third of those you visit will gladly and willingly promise to co-operate faithfully in the aims of the crusade. Another third who attend one or two Sundays each month can with comparative ease be persuaded to sign the church loyalty card. From the other third, however, you may receive comments, excuses, complaints, faultfinding, criticism, argument, and reasons, fancied or real, that will startle you. You must be neither shocked nor disturbed by these attitudes. Some of these are spiritual defense mechanisms created to avoid facing honestly Christ and one's duty. Others are irreligious smoke screens, which are laid to hide the real reasons. Still others are nothing but red herrings of argument and prejudice drawn across the path of conversation to divert you. It will be your delicate and exciting task, with the help of God and your teammate, to remove these barriers that shut your fellow members away from God and the Church.

There are two distinctions you should always make in dealing with inactive church members. The first is between the excuses that are offered and the real reasons that lie behind these excuses. Examples of the former are: "I have so many household duties Sunday morning;" "I work so hard during the week that I have to rest on Sunday;" "I have been away some Sundays visiting relatives;" and, "There are too many hypocrites in the church." Samples of the latter are: "I am ashamed of my large unpaid pledge;" "I have become careless and worldly;" "I am doing something that is wrong and sinful;" and "I play golf Sunday mornings." Among the other basic reasons for loss of interest are the letting down of personal standards and ideals, inadequate training in church membership and Christian habits, lack of pastoral care, unchristian habits, physical disability, and carelessness.

The other distinction you will make is between the temporarily inactive and the permanently inactive members. The loneliness because of bereavement, personal illness, babies to care for, and overtime employment are types of the former. Old age, invalidism, and deafness represent the latter.

These common excuses and difficulties can be dissolved. Because excuses are usually a spiritual camouflage or a mask which the mind wears to hide the real issues, you will not find them overly difficult to meet. Persuade, but never argue. Counsel constructively, and help your fellow member find the solution to his own religious problems. Accent the affirmative; avoid the negative. Helpfully answer all questions, and constantly use the authentic reasons for church loyalty and every-Sunday attendance.

Let me now show you how to handle certain difficulties in a positive, constructive, persuasive, nonargumentative way:

1. "I have so many things to do Sunday morning that I just can't seem to get ready for church." We are all busy these days, perhaps more so than we have ever been in our lives. We never finish everything we want to do, and we just have to choose the important things and give them the right of way. I personally believe that the most important thing I do on Sunday morning is to meet God in his house at the hour of worship. God gives each one of us many hours each week. I believe he expects each of us to dedicate one of these hours to him and to our church in worship. That's reasonable, isn't it? Each one of us usually finds time to do whatever he really wants to do, such as attending lodge, hearing a concert, or going out to dinner. In our home we always plan our Sunday-morning activities so that we can be at church and church school on time. You used to do that, and for the sake of your own Christian life and your church I feel sure that you will be willing, beginning this coming Sunday, to do it again.

2. "I don't like two of the members of our church." I don't either, but I do not permit them to keep me from worshiping God in my own church. In all lodges, clubs, and organizations there are many members of whose habits of life we do not approve, but we do not for that reason resign or remain away from the meetings. In a congregation the size of ours we should naturally expect to find a few we do not care for, but for every one of them there are scores and scores of good, wholesome Christians like ourselves, who are trying to do the will of God and to lead the Christian life.

Not one of us, you know, is perfect. Christ, through his Church, is trying to help all of us toward a finer, better life. You and I are really too intelligent and fine spirited to let two or three imperfect people keep us from worshiping God and serving Christ through our church. We must never blame the whole church for what one or two individuals have done. For the sake of your own Christian life just forgive and forget in the spirit of Christ, and come and be with us on all the Sundays of our loyalty crusade. You will promise to do that, I am sure.

3. *"I can attend church by radio here in my own home."* I remember when I was ill about two years ago and I heard Dr. Static preach a fairly good sermon one Sunday, while the music was quite acceptable. To me, however, it was only a substitute during sickness, and by contrast with the warmhearted, friendly services of our own church, a rather poor substitute. I missed the inspiration and spirit of our sanctuary. I missed seeing my friends before and after church. I missed joining in the hymns and sharing with my fellow members the joy of common worship. I was alone listening at long distance to the service of a church I had never attended and to a sermon by a minister I had never met. I felt all week that I had missed something rich and valuable out of my life, which only my church could give me. When you think seriously about it, you no doubt feel the same way and have probably often felt that you should begin your regular Sunday attendance again in your own church. We need you in our church, and you need us. Because of that we have called tonight, and we feel sure that you will let us take back to our pastor your promise to be present every Sunday throughout the church loyalty crusade.

And now I am going to give you workers the opportunity of telling us how you would solve some of the excuses and difficulties that you may meet. [The pastor should now choose from the twenty excuses and reasons listed on pages 77-83 those which he believes the visitors will be likely to meet.]

Keep the conversation always on the high level of agreement. After you have answered many questions, criticisms, or objections as tactfully and persuasively as you can, always return to the main objective of your visit. Always bring the mind of your prospect back to those broad foundations of our Christian faith, such as God, Christ, the value of the church, Christian ideals, and Christian character, where there is substantial and friendly agreement.

**Show how to secure a loyalty pledge.** Your own individual appeal as a friend and fellow member will often be a potent factor in the decision when expressed in words like these:

We who are your friends miss you in our work and fellowship. . . . You need the church, and your church needs you in its growing program of service. . . . Your example and influence count for Christ and the best things when you are present. . . . Your church is stronger when you are there. . . . It doesn't seem natural or right to have you away from church. . . . Let's just forget the past and begin all over again next Sunday. . . . I'll be looking for you at the great Communion service next Sunday.

Now come the promise and the signature. Visit with each prospect until you are reasonably sure that the decision will be favorable; then give him the Church Loyalty Covenant card, with a pencil, saying as you do so:

This is the Church Loyalty Covenant card, on which all of us as loyal members are indicating our willingness to cooperate in the loyalty crusade. My teammate and I have already signed ours, and we are sure that after you read it you will also gladly sign yours.

Then you may either read it aloud with your prospect or let him read it silently. You will find that practically everyone, after you have adequately presented the whole matter, will sign.

If any member has really valid reasons for not signing the card, you will of course accept the situation. If the reasons are little more than excuses, you will visit further until a promise is secured if at all possible. If you believe it is impossible to secure a definite promise, leave the card with your prospect as a last resort, with the urgent suggestion that he pray about it and bring it the following Sunday. At the close of your call you will often find it eminently appropriate to offer a brief prayer confirming the decision and asking God's blessing upon the home. As a final word of farewell as you leave for your next call, you may wish to say,

We shall eagerly look forward to seeing you next Sunday, which all of us hope to make one of the most memorable Sundays in the whole history of our church.

**Request workers to report special cases.** Because some of your fellow members will talk more freely and frankly to you than they would to their minister, you will discover many facts and attitudes about which your pastor should know. Some will offer suggestions and helpful criticisms that will benefit the church. In others you will find talents and skills which will be of great importance in building an inactive member securely into the life of the church. Still others may be sensitive about some trivial grievance that can easily be dissolved by a call from your minister. A few of the most difficult and delicate cases will be in serious need of pastoral counsel. In every case you will wish to give your minister all the facts as you see them and to offer him your best judgment concerning the best way to handle them.

God bless you as you use your best judgment as to the wisest way of handling them.

[After all the workers' questions have been answered, the pastor will close the loyalty training conference on a high note of faith and confidence in victory with prayer.]

# CHAPTER 10

# How to Use Publicity to Build Up Church Attendance

BASIC PRINCIPLES

1. It is the sacred obligation of every church to spread the good news of its services and activities.

2. Attractive publicity will help greatly in increasing attendance at improved church services.

3. A weekly church-news bulletin mailed to all members and constituents outranks every other medium of information.

4. News stories and paid advertising in the public press lift church attendance.

5. The spoken word of invitation by a loyal church member is a most effective form of publicity.

6. A church's public relations with its community are so important as to merit an adequate budget for year-round publicity.

THE public relations which your church sustains with its membership and community are of far greater importance than you may realize. What standing and reputation has your church in its neighborhood? What does your town or city know about your program of service? What does your church do to build good will toward it? How effective are the announcements of your Sunday services? Does a steady stream of interesting information concerning your church's activities and

145

achievements flow into the mind of your community through the public press? Is the general attitude one of admiration or indifference?

In a small New England city the Congregational church had for many years served a limited and increasingly exclusive clientele. Its services were quiet and dignified, while its announcements through the press were ordinary, and its program and approach to its community were largely conventional. Because the people knew little about it, they simply took it for granted and passed it by. The minister at last caught the vision of the unlimited possibilities that lay in an improved program of service announced through effective publicity. He began preaching better sermons, procured better music, strengthened the teaching force of the church school, organized a young-married-people's class, guided his youth group toward more helpful and interesting programs, had the church lawn landscaped and the church and bulletin board repainted, and selected a public relations or publicity committee. The church's light, which had been hidden under a bushel of indifference and neglect, was placed on the candlestick of publicity through news stories in the press, a well-written bulletin mailed to the members and constituency, and other opened channels of communication. Within two years this church became the most favorably known in the city, with enlarged crowds, improved morale, and increased income.

It is the sacred duty of every church to proclaim to its entire community the good news of the Son of God as expressed in the Sunday services and in the program of activities and fellowship.

**Appoint a public relations committee,** composed of three or five alert members of the congregation. One of these should be a woman and one a young person, with the most "publicity-minded" person in the church as chairman. Help this committee to explore thoroughly and objectively the church's relation to its community. Lift the news outlets already available. Consider the "good news" that should be broadcast. Determine the first three or four projects that should be undertaken. Launch those first which require little or no expenditure of funds so that the way may be paved for favorable action on the committee's later request for money. Discuss the publicity features suggested in the remaining sections of this chapter.

**Publish an attractive weekly church bulletin.** Whether neatly duplicated on inexpensive paper or elaborately printed in color with cuts, the weekly church bulletin mailed to the homes of members and constituents outranks in church-news and church-attendance values any other form of church publicity. Arriving regularly, week after week, this "house organ" brings the news of the parish and the announcement of the Sunday services of worship and preaching, with frequent emphasis on the Christian privilege and obligation of every-Sunday church attendance. Under such names as *The Outlook, The Visitor, Church News, The Chimes, The Messenger,* and *The Mirror,* this publication may be mailed, either as third-class printed matter, with a postage stamp affixed, or as second-class matter—as our daily and weekly newspapers—for a few cents a pound provided a postal permit has been secured. Full information concerning this is available at any post office in the United States.

Experience has shown that cumulative results flow from a series of church-attendance announcements appearing consecutively in the church bulletin. These appeals must be personal, brief, provocative, and direct in thought and language. They must aim at the conscience and must feature the duty as well as the privilege of every-Sunday church attendance. They must seek to convince the reason, create a sense of responsibility, and motivate the will. The following paragraphs, boxed so as to cause them to stand out, can be easily adapted to the needs of the church and to the space available:

---

#### THIS IS RALLY SUNDAY! EVERYONE PRESENT

Through your loyal attendance at the service of worship, the church school, and the young people's meetings, you can make this Rally Day the most notable our church has ever known.

The tides of interest and attendance have been higher during the month of September than in many years.

Deepen your Christian life, and lift the life of your church, by your presence on Rally Sunday and every Sunday during the year.

---

#### WORLD COMMUNION SUNDAY AND THE CHURCH LOYALTY CRUSADE

Our church loyalty crusade opens with World Communion Sunday this Sunday, when it is the privilege and duty of every member of the church to take Communion. Let us all believe and pray that it marks the beginning of the greatest year our church has known in recent history.

Your attendance and spirit in church this Sunday will bring to you the radiant life of God.

You owe to your God, to your Saviour, to your church, and to yourself your every-Sunday worship in your church.

*Every church member in church every Sunday beginning this Sunday!*

---

### I Shall Be Present Every Sunday

I resolve and promise that beginning this New Year Sunday I shall be present for worship in my church every Sunday in this new year except when prevented by illness or absence from the city.

—EVERY MEMBER OF THE CHURCH

### Your Conscience Tells You—

That you should be present in the service of your church every Sunday.

That you "feel better" when you have been in church.

That Sunday isn't properly spent unless you have been in your place of worship in your church.

That something has been lost from your life when you miss attending church.

That you have done your duty to God and to yourself only when you have met him in his house on his day.

### Excuses That Were Not Offered

"I worked hard all week and was tired Sunday morning, but I am always rested and refreshed by my every-Sunday attendance at the services of my church."

"I had company come for Sunday dinner, so I brought them along to church for the morning service. They greatly enjoyed and appreciated it."

"I had been to a party very late Saturday night, but I never permit my social enjoyment to interfere with my religious duties. Of course, I was in church Sunday morning."

"It was just impossible last Sunday morning to get to church, so of course I attended the evening service. It was interesting and helpful."

### I GET THE LIFT I NEED AT CHURCH

One's life and faith tend to sag under the heavy burden which the workaday world lays upon one.

Freed from these burdens on the Lord's Day, one finds at the hour of worship the inspiration, strength, confidence, and vision that everyone sorely needs.

Peace instead of tension, faith in place of fear, and God rather than gold provide a sanctuary for the soul.

### PROSPER THE WORK OF GOD

You do not prosper, nor does your church, when you are absent from its services on Sunday.

Your friends miss you; you miss your friends.

God misses the chance of whispering his love and showing his plans to you.

The strangers you might have greeted with a welcome do not see your smile or feel the friendliness of your handshake.

When you are present every Sunday, everything goes well!

Leaflets on church attendance should be provided for distribution at the church services, for mailing, and for your church pamphlet rack. Some extremely persuasive pamphlets on the privilege, benefits, and duty of every-Sunday church attendance are available from the denominational boards of evangelism, such as *Resolved, Why I Go to Church, My Church,* and *Ten Reasons for Attending Church.* Excerpts from these pamphlets are often printed in the weekly bulletin as a stimulus in forming the habit of church attendance, credit of course being given to the source of the quotation.

The post office offers many other opportunities. Well-written letters and printed, or neatly duplicated, postal cards present very attractive methods of building church attendance through direct-mail advertising, especially for special events and seasons such as Christmas, Lent, Holy Week, and Easter.

**Write interesting reports for local newspapers.** In community-wide coverage the local press outranks every other medium of effective publicity. Because it enters the home of churchmen and nonchurchmen alike, it offers an open door to the mind of the community.

The large majority of newspapers are friendly to the religious groups of the community and are eager to serve them. Most editors will gladly—within the limits of space available to them—print news stories announcing the services and sermon subjects of any church provided these stories are really news and are well written.

A good news story is one that has news value; deals with an event of interest; catches the interest of the reader in the first few words; includes the names and correct initials of people participating in the event, with interesting information about them; lists features that attract; is neatly typewritten, double spaced, on one side of a sheet of paper; and is handed in on time.

A conventional, dull, and rather uninteresting announcement for a patriotic World Order Sunday service read as follows:

Dr. John Jones will preach Sunday morning at the usual hour in First Church on the subject "The Kind of a World I Should Like to Live in." Special music has been arranged.

A well-written news article about this same event, with real pulling power, would read:

"The Kind of a World I Should Like to Live in" is the World Order sermon subject on which Dr. John Jones will preach at the eleven o'clock service next Sunday morning in First Church. Having traveled extensively in Europe after the First World War, and having served as chaplain in the Pacific during the Second World War, Dr. Jones brings a background of experience and patriotic service to his message concerning the building of an enduring world peace.

The members of the American Legion will be special guests of honor, sitting in pews reserved for them. Four service men who are members of the First Church—Robert James, Douglas Beers, John Merwin, and Richard Meier— will act as ushers. Patriotic decorations, which include flags of the allied nations, are under the charge of Mrs. Henry Johnson.

The appropriate music will include Kipling's "Recessional," by the chorus choir under the direction of Austin Truitt, while a baritone solo "The Dawn of a New World" will be sung by Earl Parr. The singing of "The Star-Spangled Banner" will close the service. The public is cordially invited.

Newsworthy excerpts from your Sunday sermon may appear in Monday papers if you carefully select and report them. Most parts of a good sermon have little or no news value. They deal with the great Christian truths that are valid for life but uninteresting to newspaper readers. Other portions of nearly every sermon have a present-day application to current problems that will help them easily find their way, under proper guidance, into the Monday edition of the daily press. When the controversial and the provocative are discussed in good taste and in a sound and creative way, the minister will find that his sermon is not only news but an instrument in helping him mold the thinking and conviction of his community. Sermon excerpts or paragraphs that have news value should always be typewritten, double spaced, in duplicate, and on one side of a plain sheet of paper. Reputable newspapers prefer a written report to one given over the phone, where misunderstanding and misquotation can so easily and unintentionally occur. An example of good reporting is this article, which appeared one Monday morning in the *New York Times:*

## SERVICE BY MAN STRESSED

### Elliott Says We Are Most Loyal When We Have Sacrificed

A "well-rounded" Christian experience implies an awareness of "not simply what Christ has done for us, but also what we can do for Him," the Rev. Dr. Phillips P. Elliott, pastor of the First Presbyterian Church, Henry and Clark Streets, Brooklyn, said yesterday in his sermon.

"We are most loyal to the persons or causes for which we have sacrificed the most," he asserted. "With full awareness of what Christ has done for us we need now to stress more vigorously what we can do for Him. In this, as in other respects, we simply emulate His experiences. His joy was in serving man and our joy should be not simply acceptance of that service, but should reveal an equivalent concern for Him and for one another.

"So the nations of the world today, and particularly our own country, will be drawn closer to one another if they are concerned not simply in giving to meet others' needs, but also in receiving from others those unique gifts which each land is qualified to bestow."

Sermon subjects should always be phrased to have pulling power. "Your sermon subject interested me, and I came to hear what you had to say about it," said a widely read, thoughtful community leader of no church affiliation to a Presbyterian minister. Sermon subjects can have both publicity value and pulling power. They can be arresting, intriguing, and magnetic without being sensational, freakish, or bizarre. A good sermon title is always truthful, concise, positive, descriptive, and religious. It stirs hope and intrigues interest. It never raises doubt.

Many ministers phrase the title of each sermon in four or five different ways, choosing the one that is most honest and persuasive. In preaching recently on prayer, one preacher chose "The Power of Prayer" as his sermon title, instead of "Prayer in a World of Law and Science," "Does Prayer Accomplish Anything?" "Is It Worth While Praying?" or "Why Pray?" Attractively announced in the newspaper, as well as on the bulletin board and in the weekly calendar, a good sermon subject helps bring people to church.

Churches whose financial resources permit find that a regular "ad" on the church page more than justifies the expense. Their experience checks with that of commercial concerns, which spend almost fabulous sums in newspaper and radio advertising to keep their names and their wares before the public. Churches that cannot afford to purchase space each week find that the seasonal appeals of Thanksgiving, Christmas, Lent, Palm Sunday, and Easter presented in large display ads will usually pay for themselves through increased attendance.

A well-written church advertisement always has the twofold purpose of drawing people to the services advertised and keeping the name of the church before the community. The features that attract should stand out in blackfaced type with an ample amount of white space around it. While an ad should not be too crowded, it is generally true that "the more you tell, the more you sell." The following display seems to meet most of the conditions of excellence and effectiveness:

---

## THE BAPTIST TEMPLE
North and Franklin Sts.
### THE REV. ALBERT M. McCARTNEY, MINISTER
**Sermon 11:00 A. M.  "A DEDICATED LIFE"**
Church School 10:00 A. M.          Youth Groups 4:00, 6:30 P. M.

**Attract those who pass by.** Among the usual opportunities are the following:

*Make the outdoor bulletin board speak.* An attractive bulletin board properly placed on the church lawn or permanently attached to the edifice itself will probably invite more people to church than most other publicity devices. Bearing the name of the church and minister, it announces the Sunday services and weekday activities to all who pass. It displays messages such as those provided by *The Wayside Pulpit*, while it serves as a silent, constant reminder of one's duty to God and his church. Boards of varying sizes with glass doors and electrical illumination either can be purchased from a denominational supply house or can be built locally. In one congregation a carpenter and a local electrician took genuine pride in producing, at a total cost of the materials only, a handsome, electrically-lighted bulletin board three feet by six feet, set between iron posts on the church lawn. Loose letters of varying sizes and color can be purchased, while a letter poster done in color by some member of the church and placed in the bulletin board will heighten the pulling power of any announcement. Blessed is the sexton who keeps the announcements up to date!

*Floodlight your stained-glass windows and your church tower* so that the color and symbolism of things religious may stand out against the night and the sky.

*Broadcast chimes and music* from the bell tower of your church as increasing hundreds of churches are doing. A counted vote in the morning congregation of the City Temple in Chicago showed 26 per cent of the worshipers present came because they had heard the church chimes and hymn tunes that were broadcast by loud speakers before the service. In nearly every congregation some generous well-to-do member can be found who will gladly present an electronic broadcasting system for broadcasting both chimes and hymns to the community.

**Employ personal contacts and messages**—from both pastor and members. Members will extend verbal invitations to acquaintances and friends. The most effective kind of attendance publicity is the personal invitation of the loyal member (the satisfied customer), who commends his church (the article) to his friend (the prospective customer) and persuades him to attend (the sale). Many members of the church, if reminded with an encouraging word from time to time, will invite their acquaintances and friends to church with words like these, as does an able insurance man:

If you are not a member of a church in our community, I should like to invite you to visit us in First Church next Sunday. We have a fine, friendly congregation, and you quite likely will meet some of your acquaintances there. Our services are always helpful, and I am sure you will enjoy hearing Dr. Smith, our minister. He has something worth while to say and says it well. Our service is at eleven o'clock, and I shall be glad either to meet you at the church or to call at your home for you at about a quarter of eleven. My wife and I would like to have you sit with us and meet a number of our friends. Would you care to have me do this either this Sunday or the following one?

The minister can telephone a cordial invitation to nonattending members. Next to a personal pastoral call a friendly telephone conversation will produce gratifying results in renewing interest among inactive members. The wise pastor will never reprove, criticize, or find fault with, the nonattending member. He will rather telephone as a friend, beginning with words like these:

I was just thinking of you, as I had missed you from church last Sunday, and I thought I would phone to inquire if anyone was ill. We had a splendid congregation last Sunday and a very helpful service. I just wanted you to know that I had missed you, and I am sure you missed being with us in our service of worship. I'm making a special effort to encourage every member of our church to be present every Sunday, except when illness or absence from the city prevents. I always appreciate your presence there, as folks like you challenge and help me to do my best. I also called to inquire if you have among your acquaintances anyone who is a prospective member for our church. I shall be glad to call on him and help you win him.

The telephone ranks as one of the least-used, but simplest, devices for building church attendance. One minister whose lameness prevented him from making pastoral calls preached to the largest congregation in a city of twenty thousand. He attributed his success, first, to the fact that he always prepares the best possible service and sermons and, second, to his making over fifty telephone calls each week.

New residents in your community will appreciate being invited to attend your church. The most propitious time for interesting new residents in visiting your church is immediately after they arrive in the community. Because they are lonesome and usually friendless, they respond more readily to a cordial invitation to attend church and church school than they do at any other time. A personal letter, such as the one on page 158, signed by the minister has been used effectively in small and large cities to attract newcomers to church services. Followed by a personal call by the minister or some friendly neighbor, this letter paves the way for a goodly percentage of church accessions among newcomers in a community.

My dear Mr. and Mrs. Smith:

I just learned of your moving into our community and wish to add my welcome to those you have already received. You will very soon sense the fine community spirit, the civic pride, and the close co-operation among the churches of our city.

When you are settled in your new home, you will wish to look about for a church home. You will find nearly every denomination represented in our city with strong churches, able ministers, and friendly members.

May I cordially urge you to associate yourselves with the church of your choice at the earliest possible moment.

If you have no other denominational preference, I should be happy to have you visit our church next Sunday. The enclosed bulletin will tell you something of our services, sermons, church school, and youth groups.

First Church is located at the corner of Main and Church Streets, and is easily accessible from all parts of the city. Should you later move to some other neighborhood in the community, you would still find our church easily reached by auto or bus.

I hope you have a most satisfactory and long residence in our city.

Very sincerely yours,

(Signed by the Minister)

## A Growing Congregation

Every church can have a growing congregation.

Every minister who enriches his church's services, and who improves his sermons, can preach to a growing congregation. Through a persistent, intelligent program of education and publicity every church can markedly increase its attendance. Renewed interest, enriched spiritual life, larger collections, and increased numbers will make the harvest of achievement an abundant one.

*God wills it! It can be done!*

# INDEX